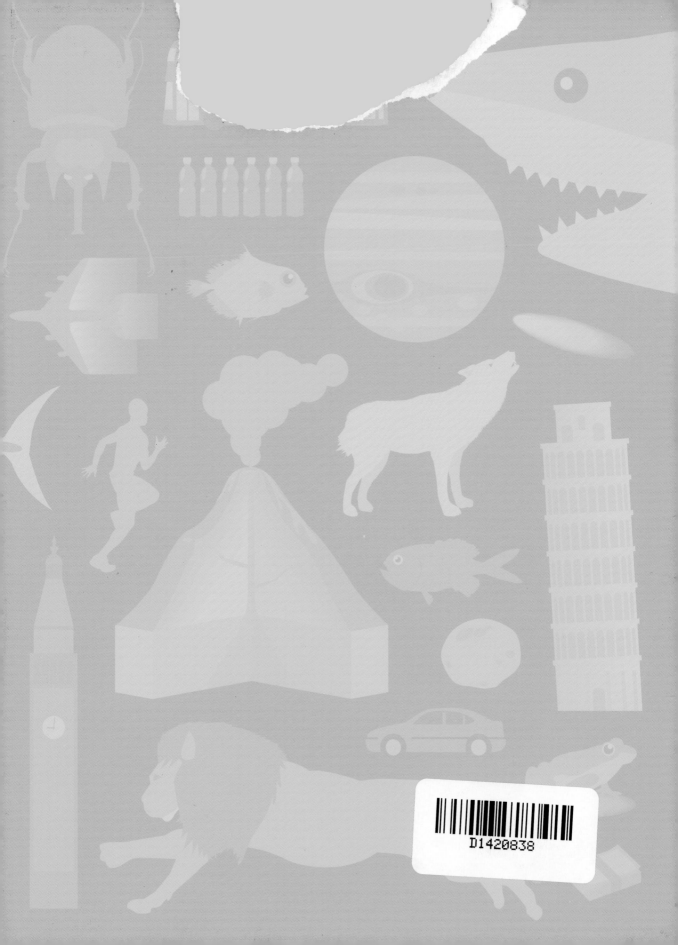

INFOMANIA

AWESOME RECORDS, TOP 10s & FACTS

WAYLAND

First published in 2015 by Wayland
The edition published in 2016

Copyright © Wayland 2015

The material in this book has previously been published in the
following titles: *Infographic Top 10: Record-breaking Buildings,
Infographic Top 10: Record-breaking Animals, Infographic Top
10: Record-breaking Earth & Space* and *Infographic Top 10:
Record-breaking Humans.*

Original series produced by Tall Tree Ltd
Interior Design: Alyssa Peacock
Cover Design: Graham Saville
Editorial Consultant: Hayley Fairhead
Editor: Corinne Lucas

ISBN: 978 0 7502 9891 9

10 9 8 7 6 5 4 3 2 1

Wayland
An imprint of Hachette Children's Group
Part of Hodder and Stoughton
Carmelite House
50 Victoria Embankment
London, EC4Y 0DZ

An Hachette UK Company

www.hachette.co.uk
www.hachettechildrens.co.uk

Printed in Malaysia

CONTENTS

CONTENTS

WELCOME!

⟨‹ ·· ›⟩

From the deadliest animal to the closest star, from the tallest building to the fastest human, this book looks at amazing record-breakers in our Universe. It uses stunning icons, graphics and visualisations to show you the extremes of human endeavour, space and the natural world.

pages 46–47
See what is inside a volcano and discover how violent a volcanic eruption can be.

pages 70–71
Discover how fast the world's quickest rollercoasters can travel.

pages 16–17
See which birds have the largest wings and how they use them.

pages 68–69
Measure the world's largest book next to a giraffe.

SPEED ACROSS THE GROUND

Some animals have evolved the amazing ability to run at breath-taking speed. Many of them can sprint short distances to chase down prey, while others can run fast to outpace and dodge any chasing predators.

Galloping horses

Fast-running, four-legged animals use their legs in sequence to push themselves as fast as possible. A horse's gallop begins with the two back feet pushing off the ground, one after the other. For a short period, the horse is off the ground, before the front two legs touch down.

FASTEST LAND ANIMALS

1. **Cheetah 120 km/h**
2. Pronghorn 88.5 km/h
3. **Springbok 88 km/h**
4. Wildebeest 80.5 km/h
5. **Lion 80 km/h**
6. Greyhound 74 km/h
7. **Jackrabbit 72 km/h**
=8. African wild dog 71 km/h
=8. **Kangaroo 71 km/h**
10. Horse 70 km/h

Fastest human: 44.7 km/h recorded during a 100-m-sprint (average speed 10.44 metres per second) by Usain Bolt.

Extending strides

Cheetahs are the sprint kings of the animal world. They have lightweight, slim bodies, which are perfect for life in the fast lane. Another key feature is a very flexible spine. This allows the cheetah to take enormous strides, each up to 8 m long, making it incredibly fast.

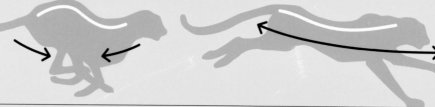

Spine compressed

Spine extended

ON THE RUN

The world's fastest sprinters can run at 45 km/h, but they can only manage this pace for a short time. Other runners need more endurance than speed to take part in races that cross deserts or climb skyscrapers.

In just **four years**, two Jamaican sprinters managed to set **five** new world 100-m records.

100-m record progression

16 August 2009

16 August 2008

31 May 2008

9 September 2007

14 June 2005

| 9.5 | 9.6 | 9.7 | 9.8 | 9.9 | 10 |

9.58 seconds

9.69 seconds

9.72 seconds

9.74 seconds

9.77 seconds

←------------ Usain Bolt ------------→ ←------ Asafa Powell ------→

How far in 10 seconds?

These bars show the distance a sprinter, a marathon runner, a record-breaking swimmer and a person moving at normal walking pace could cover in 10 seconds.

Olympic sprinter – 100 m

Marathon runner – 57.15 m

Olympic swimmer – 24 m

Walking pace – 16 m

←------------------- **10 seconds** -------------------→

RUNNING RECORDS

1. **100 metres: Usain Bolt (Jamaica) – 9.58 secs**

2. 110 metre hurdles: Aries Merritt (USA) – 12.8 secs

3. **200 metres: Usain Bolt (Jamaica) – 19.19 secs**

4. 400 metres: Michael Johnson (USA) – 43.18 secs

5. **800 metres: David Lekuta Rudisha (Kenya) – 1 min 40.91 secs**

6. 1,500 metres: Hicham El Guerrouj (Morocco) – 3 mins 26 secs

7. **5,000 metres: Kenenisa Bekele (Ethiopia) – 12 mins 37.35 secs**

8. 10,000 metres: Kenenisa Bekele (Ethiopia) – 26 mins 17.53 secs

9. **Half marathon: Zersenay Tadese (Eritrea) – 58 mins 23 secs**

10. Marathon: Dennis Kimetto (Kenya) – 2 hours 2 mins 57 secs

Ultra Marathon

Ultra-marathon runner Marshall Ulrich ran **4,930 km** from San Francisco to New York in just **52 days**. That is nearly **95 km** every day!

San Francisco

New York

At the 1896

Olympic Games in Athens, Spiridon Louis of Greece won the gold medal in the marathon, completing the race in a time of 2 hours, 58 minutes, 50 seconds.

86th floor

320 m

MARATHON DES SABLES

Competitors in the Marathon des Sables have to run 251 km (that's the same as running 9.5 marathons!) across the north African desert in six days, experiencing temperatures over 50°C.

Empire State

Every year, more than **400 athletes** race up the Empire State Building in New York City. They have to run up to the **86th floor**, climbing **1,576 steps** on the way. The winner usually completes the race in a little over **10 minutes**.

SPEED IN THE WATER

It is much harder to move quickly through water than air, because water is far more dense. To swim quickly, super-fast fish need to have sleek, streamlined bodies and amazingly strong muscles.

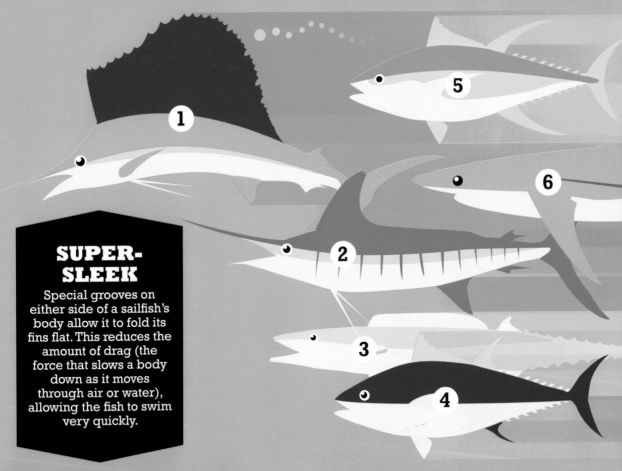

SUPER-SLEEK

Special grooves on either side of a sailfish's body allow it to fold its fins flat. This reduces the amount of drag (the force that slows a body down as it moves through air or water), allowing the fish to swim very quickly.

How far in 1 second?

This chart shows how far these different animals can swim in a single second compared to humans.

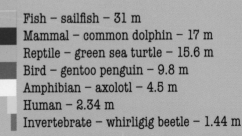

Fish – sailfish – 31 m
Mammal – common dolphin – 17 m
Reptile – green sea turtle – 15.6 m
Bird – gentoo penguin – 9.8 m
Amphibian – axolotl – 4.5 m
Human – 2.34 m
Invertebrate – whirligig beetle – 1.44 m

FASTEST SWIMMING ANIMALS

1. **Sailfish 112 km/h**
2. Striped marlin 80 km/h
3. **Wahoo 77 km/h**
4. Southern blue fin tuna 76 km/h
5. **Yellow fin tuna 74 km/h**
6. Blue shark 69 km/h
=7. **Bonefish 64 km/h**
=7. Swordfish 64 km/h
9. **Tarpon 56 km/h**
10. Tiger shark 53 km/h

Humans can swim at 8.45 km/h. This is the average speed of an Olympic 50-m freestyle swimmer.

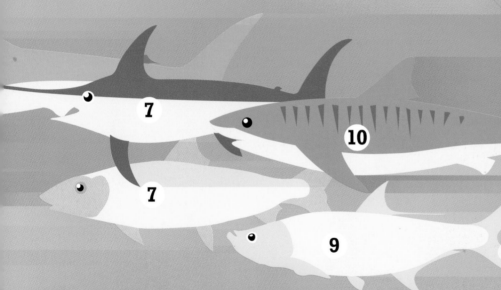

Convergent evolution

Fish have fins to push and steer them through the water. Other animals have body parts that look and work like fins – swimming birds have fin-shaped wings, while swimming mammals have flippers. The development of similar body parts by different animals is called convergent evolution.

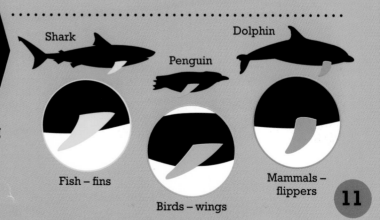

Shark

Penguin

Dolphin

Fish – fins

Birds – wings

Mammals – flippers

SWIMMING AND DIVING

Some deep divers use a line and a weighted sled to carry them down.

Take a deep breath and plunge beneath the surface with these amazing water sport records. These can involve diving from a great height, plunging to the ocean's depths or racing through a swimming pool.

Free diving

←---- 100 m ----→

←------------ 281 m ------------→

Dynamic apnea with fins involves swimming as far as possible **underwater** on one breath. The record is held by Goran Colak from Croatia, and it is **281 m** – that's nearly three football pitches.

Deepest dive

Herbert Nitsch of Austria dived to a depth of **214 m** and returned to the surface on a single breath! That's more than twice the height of the **Statue of Liberty**.

214 m

93 m

Diving

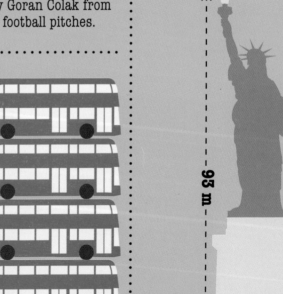

Cliff divers jump off a platform that's 27 m above the water – as tall as a nine storey building.

27 m

The highest board at an indoor diving competition is 10 m high – **twice the height of a double-decker bus.**

SWIMMING RECORDS

1. **50 m freestyle:** Cesar Cielo (Brazil) – 20.91 secs

2. **50 m breaststroke:** Adam Peaty (UK) – 26.42 secs

3. **50 m backstroke:** Liam Tancock (UK) – 24.04 secs

4. **50 m butterfly:** Rafael Munoz (Spain) – 22.43 secs

5. **100 m freestyle:** Cesar Cielo (Brazil) – 46.91 secs

6. **100 m breaststroke:** Adam Peaty (UK) – 57.92 secs

7. **100 m backstroke:** Aaron Peirsol (USA) – 51.94 secs

8. **100 m butterfly:** Michael Phelps (USA) – 49.82 secs

9. **4 x 100 m freestyle:** USA – 3 mins 8.24 secs

10. **4 x 100 m medley:** USA – 3 mins 27.28 secs

Longest unassisted swim

Chloe McCardel of Australia swam for **42 hours** and covered **142 km** – more than **four times** the distance across the English Channel.

142 km
in 42 hours

England

English ::Channel

France

Swimming strokes

There are four types of **stroke** used at swimming competitions: freestyle (or front crawl), backstroke, breaststroke and butterfly. **Medleys** are a special type of race where swimmers use all four styles, one after the other.

freestyle

backstroke

breaststroke

butterfly

THROWING AND JUMPING

Power, speed and agility are vital to smash throwing and jumping records. Throwers will try to go farther than anyone before, while jumpers will go for distance and height to become world record holders.

Standing jumps

The **standing** high jump and long jump appeared at the Olympic games until 1912. Athletes tried to jump as **high** or as **long** as they could from a standing start. Today, competitors take a **run-up** before jumping.

Record distance – 3.73 m

Standing long jump

Record height – 1.9 m

Standing high jump

Throwing records

GRAPE THROW AND CATCH
A J Henderson managed to throw a **grape**, run and catch it in his mouth over a distance of 21.18 m, which is about the length of two buses.

LIGHT BULB
A **light bulb** was thrown for a record 32.53 m by Bipin Larkin.

10 m

0 m

THROWING AND JUMPING RECORDS

1. **Javelin: Jan Zelezny (Czech Republic) 25 May 1996 – 98.48 m**

2. Discus: Jürgen Schult (East Germany) 6 June 1986 – 74.08 m

3. **Hammer: Yuriy Sedykh (USSR) 30 August 1986 – 86.74 m**

4. Shot put: Randy Barnes (USA) 20 May 1990 – 23.12 m

5. **Long jump: Mike Powell (USA) 30 August 1991 – 8.95 m**

6. Pole vault: Renaud Lavillenie (France) 15 February 2014 – 6.16 m

7. **Triple jump: Jonathan Edwards (UK) 7 August 1995 – 18.29 m**

8. Standing high jump: Jonas Huusom (Denmark) 27 August 2011 – 1.48 m

9. **High jump: Javier Sotomayor (Cuba) 27 July 1993 – 2.45 m**

10. Standing long jump: Arne Tvervaag (Norway) 11 November 1968 – 3.71 m

High jump styles

Over the years, athletes have used and developed different high jump styles. Today's jumpers use the **Fosbury flop**, developed by Dick Fosbury in 1965.

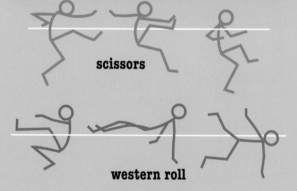

scissors

straddle

western roll

Fosbury flop

LONGEST PEANUT THROW
Former world champion hurdler Colin Jackson holds the record for the longest **peanut** throw, at 37.92 m.

EGG THROW AND CATCH
This record is held by Willie O'Donevan and Warren McElhone, and stands at 71.2 m.

BIGGEST WINGSPAN

How birds soar

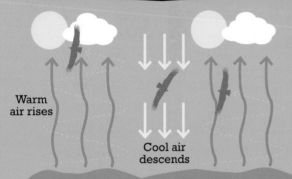

Warm air rises

Cool air descends

Many birds use their elongated wings to catch rising currents of warm air, called thermals, to push them high into the air. From here, the birds look out for signs of another thermal, before gliding over to it so they can be pushed up again.

=5 Bearded vulture

Bearded vultures are found throughout mountainous regions of Europe, Africa, and Asia.

3 metres

=7 Griffon vulture

These birds live in colonies high up on cliffs. From here, they can fly out and search for dead animals to feed on.

2.8 metres

=7 California condor

The California condor uses rising air currents to soar up to altitudes of 4,500 m or more.

2.8 metres

=9 Golden eagle

These birds build huge nests, which are known as eyries.

2.5 metres

=9 Grey crowned crane

These birds use large inflatable sacs beneath their chins to produce loud, booming calls.

2.5 metres

Marabou stork

=3

Marabou storks feed mainly on dead animals, but they will catch live prey during the breeding season.

3.4 metres

Wandering albatross

=1

These giant birds use their enormous wings to glide over the ocean for hours without having to flap them.

3.6 metres

Whooper swan

=5

These birds migrate for hundreds of kilometres in large 'V' formations.

3 metres

Andean condor

=3

These heavy birds can weigh up to 15 kg and need thermals or winds to help them into the air.

3.4 metres

Great white pelican

=1

A great white pelican will eat up to 1.5 kg of fish every single day.

3.6 metres

LOUDEST ANIMALS

<——· · · · · · · · · · · · · · · ——>

Some whales can produce sounds that could travel more than 2,600 km in ideal conditions. That's almost the distance from Chicago to Los Angeles. However, modern noise pollution limits this distance.

LOUD BANG

By clicking one of its claws, a tiger pistol shrimp creates a 'bubble bullet' that bursts and stuns prey. The extreme pressure caused by the bubble also creates a flash of light indicating very high temperatures. Scientists believe the temperature inside the bubble can reach nearly 5,500°C – that's as hot as the surface of the Sun!

1 ## Tiger pistol shrimp

This tiny crustacean makes the loudest noise in the animal world as it clicks its claws.

200dB

dB

0

80

20 40 60

SILENCE

A WHISPER

NORMAL CONVERSATION

200

2 ## Blue whale

The largest animal on the planet makes low frequency sounds which scientists believe are used to attract mates.

188 dB

190

Echolocation

Echoes bounce back

VOLCANO ERUPTION

180

ROCKET LAUNCH

170

160

Some animals, such as dolphins and bats, use sounds to detect prey. They send out high-pitched sounds, called ultrasound, which bounce back off any prey, telling the predator where its prey is.

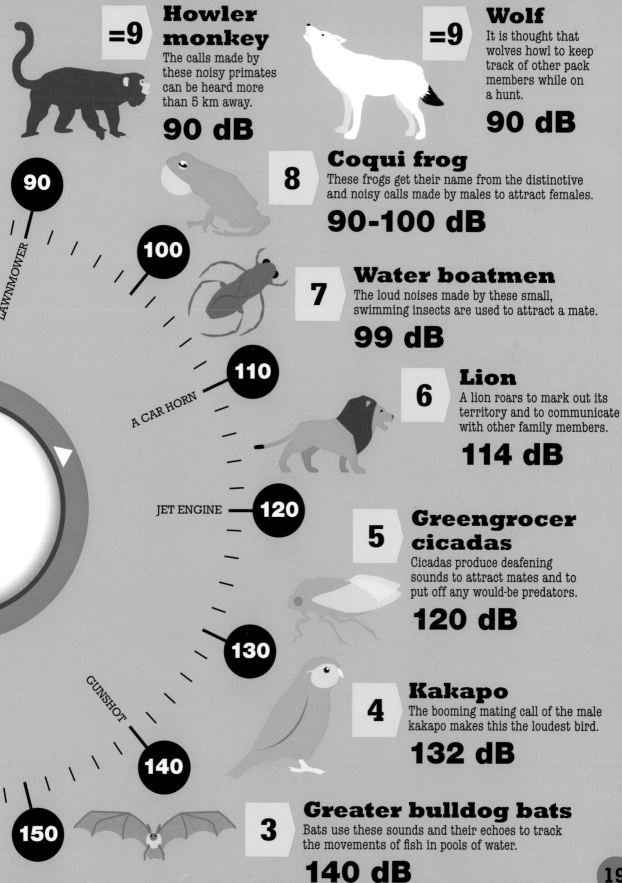

Howler monkey

=9

The calls made by these noisy primates can be heard more than 5 km away.

90 dB

Wolf

=9

It is thought that wolves howl to keep track of other pack members while on a hunt.

90 dB

Coqui frog

8

These frogs get their name from the distinctive and noisy calls made by males to attract females.

90-100 dB

Water boatmen

7

The loud noises made by these small, swimming insects are used to attract a mate.

99 dB

Lion

6

A lion roars to mark out its territory and to communicate with other family members.

114 dB

Greengrocer cicadas

5

Cicadas produce deafening sounds to attract mates and to put off any would-be predators.

120 dB

Kakapo

4

The booming mating call of the male kakapo makes this the loudest bird.

132 dB

Greater bulldog bats

3

Bats use these sounds and their echoes to track the movements of fish in pools of water.

140 dB

LAWNMOWER

90

100

A CAR HORN

110

JET ENGINE

120

130

GUNSHOT

140

150

NASTY GNASHERS!

The hardest parts of your body are your teeth. These tough mouth parts are designed to tear off food and crush it up so that our bodies can absorb nutrients. Animals also use their teeth for fighting and killing prey.

Teeth types

Animal teeth can be long and pointed for fighting and grasping, sharp like scissors for slicing through meat, or flat and tough to grind up plant food.

Molars
These are used for grinding food.

Tusks
Tusks are teeth that are so long, they stick out of the mouth. They are used for fighting and rummaging for food.

Carnassials
Carnivores have these scissor-like teeth for slicing through meat and bone.

Canines
Located at the front of the mouth, these long, sharp teeth are used to grasp prey.

Snake fangs

Some snakes kill their prey by injecting them with a deadly venom, delivered through needle-sharp fangs. The long fangs have a canal running through them. As the snake bites into its prey, venom is pushed through these canals and into the victim's body.

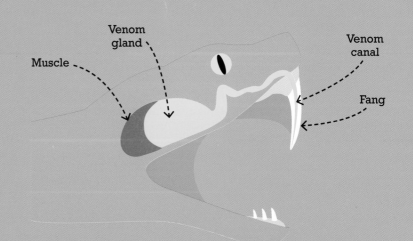

Venom gland

Venom canal

Muscle

Fang

20

LONGEST ANIMAL TEETH

1. **African elephant tusks – 3 m**
2. **Narwhal tusk – 2.7 m**
3. **Asian elephant tusks – 2.4 m**
4. **Walrus tusks – 90 cm**
5. **Hippopotamus teeth – 40 cm**
6. **Babirusa tusks – 30 cm**
7. **Warthog tusks – 25.5 cm**
8. **Sperm whale teeth – 18 cm**
9. **Payara fangs – 15 cm**
10. **Lion canines – 9 cm**

The longest human tooth measured 3.2 cm. It was extracted from the mouth of Loo Hui Jing of Singapore in 2009.

Animals with the most teeth

A human child usually has 24 teeth, and an adult will replace these with 32 teeth.

The record for the human with the most teeth was a boy in India who had 232 extracted in 2014.

But even this is nothing compared to the record-breakers of the animal kingdom.

Sharks can have 20,000 teeth throughout their life – they are replaced regularly.

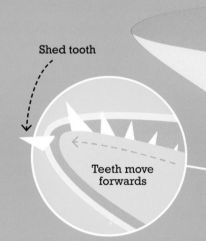

Shed tooth

Teeth move forwards

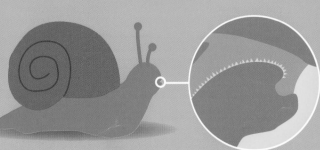

Snails have more than 25,000 tiny microscopic teeth, known as radula.

SUPER CELLS

<·····················>

The trillions of cells in your body come in all shapes and sizes. The largest are just visible to the naked eye, while the longest stretch the whole length of your legs. Together, these amazing cells create tissues that form the building blocks of your body.

Largest and smallest cells

The largest human cell is the egg or ovum. One of these can measure about 1 mm across.
The smallest cell is the sperm, which measures about **0.06 mm** long – about 10 could fit on the full stop at the end of this sentence.

6

5

7   8

10

9

4

Motor neurone

The **longest cells** in the human body are motor neurones that stretch from the base of the **spine** to muscles in the **toes**.

Longest cell

They can be up to 1 m long.

22

LONGEST BONES IN THE HUMAN BODY
(AVERAGE LENGTH – CM)

1. **Femur (thigh bone) – 50.5**
2. **Tibia (shin bone) – 42.9**
3. **Fibula (lower leg) – 40.4**
4. **Humerus (upper arm) – 36.6**
5. **Ulna (inner lower arm) – 28.2**
6. **Radius (outer lower arm) – 26.4**
7. **Seventh rib – 24.4**
8. **Eighth rib – 23.1**
9. **Innominate bone (hip bone) – 18.5**
10. **Sternum (breast bone) – 17.0**

Magnified x 70

Egg

Sperm

1

2

3

Long leg

The leg of an adult human is just under **1 m** long.

In comparison, a giraffe's leg is nearly twice as long, about **1.8 m** in length.

40%
Skeletal muscle makes up about 40 per cent of your body's mass.

In an adult weighing 70 kg, **28 kg** of that weight is muscle, which is more than the weight of **two gold bars.**

Muscle tissue

ORGANS AND SYSTEMS

The largest, heaviest organ in your body covers you completely, protecting you from the outside world. Your other organs perform an amazing range of tasks, allowing you to live, grow and survive.

Brain bits

The cerebrum is the upper portion of the brain and is its largest part, making up about ...

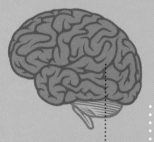

... 85% of the brain's mass.

The brain is the fattest organ in the human body.

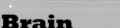

About 60% of the brain is fat.

9 Thyroid
This butterfly-shaped organ is found in your neck and produces several chemicals that tell your body how to behave.

35 g

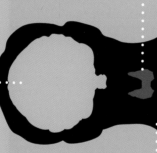

4 Lungs
These large sacs fill with air when you breathe in so that oxygen passes into your body and carbon dioxide passes out.

1,090 g

3 Brain
Protected by your skull, this organ receives signals from all over your body, and weighs as much as two basketballs.

1,263 g

5 Heart
This muscular organ is part of the blood, or circulatory, system. It weighs a little less than a tin of soup.

315 g

Thick-skinned

Skin is usually 1–2 mm thick. The thinnest parts of your skin are your eyelids (about 0.5 mm thick), while parts of the upper back have skin that is 5 mm thick.

1–2 mm

0.5 mm

5 mm

Your body has about **5.6 litres of blood**, equivalent to 5.6 litre bottles of water. This blood is pushed by the heart through the body **three times every minute**.

In one day, the blood travels a total of **19,000 km** – that is four times the distance across the **US**, from coast to coast.

4

Blood system facts

7 Spleen

This organ acts as a blood reserve. It also removes old red blood cells and helps the immune system.

170 g

8 Pancreas

This organ produces chemicals which tell your body how to act, as well enzymes, which break down food.

98 g

1 Skin

This organ covers your entire body and prevents water loss. It weighs about as much as four bricks.

10,886 g

Your stomach

is a stretchy bag of muscle that gets bigger and smaller as food enters and leaves it. An adult stomach can expand to hold up to 1.5 litres of food.

6 Kidneys

These two organs lie on either side of your back. They filter your blood, removing harmful waste products.

290 g

2 Liver

Part of your digestive system, this organ helps you to break down and process what you eat.

1,560 g

10 Prostate

This small, walnut-size male organ makes seminal fluid, which sperm cells travel in.

20 g

SUPER STRONG

These people are the strongest on the planet! They can lift, pull and carry enormous weights, many times their own body weight, and regularly take part in competitions to see who is the strongest.

Weightlifting techniques

Breaking **power lifting** and **weightlifting** records involves trying to lift as much as possible using the techniques shown here.

Snatch

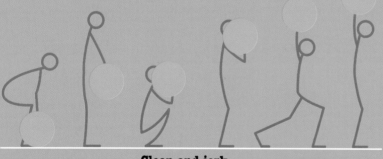

Clean and jerk

Deadlift

Squat

Bench press

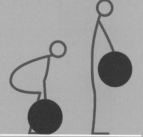

Lance Karabel of the USA holds the record for the squat, carrying 455 kg – that's almost the same as the weight of an adult male grizzly bear.

Dariusz Slowik from Poland threw a **48-kg** washing machine a distance of **3.5 m** to set a new record.

POWER & WEIGHTLIFTING RECORDS

1. **Snatch (men): Behdad Salimkordasiabi (Iran) – 214 kg**

2. **Clean and jerk (men): Aleksey Lovchev (Russia) – 264 kg**

3. **Combined (snatch and clean and jerk) (men): Aleksey Lovchev (Russia) – 475 kg**

4. **Snatch (women): Tatiana Kashirina (Russia) – 155 kg**

5. **Clean and jerk (women): Tatiana Kashirina (Russia) – 193 kg**

6. **Combined snatch and clean and jerk (women): Tatiana Kashirina (Russia) – 348 kg**

7. **Squat: Andrey Malanichev (Russia) – 470 kg**

8. **Bench press: Kirill Sarychev (Russia) – 335 kg**

9. **Dead lift: Eddie Hall (UK) – 463 kg**

10. **Combined squat, bench press, dead lift: Lance Karabel (USA) – 1,095 kg**

World's strongest

Brian Shaw of the USA has won the World's Strongest Man Competition three times, in 2011, 2013 and 2015. Aneta Florczyk of Poland, holds the women's record with four wins. Here are some of the events that competitors take part in.

Overhead log lift

Farmer's Walk

Atlas stones

Vehicle pull

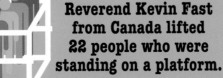

Reverend Kevin Fast from Canada lifted 22 people who were standing on a platform.

Manjit Singh

Manjit Singh of the UK pulled a double-decker London bus weighing **8 tonnes** (about the same as 1.5 elephants) **21.2 m** using ribbons tied to his hair.

He holds more than **30 strength records**, including pulling a bus with **54 people** on board with one hand.

He also pulled a **Vulcan jet bomber** weighing in at **92 tonnes** (the same as 18.5 elephants) a distance of **15 cm** using a harness.

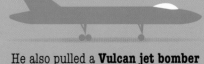

LIVING LONG

With improvements in medicine and diet, it is now not uncommon for someone in a rich country to live 100 years or more. However, there are still many poor countries where people have low life expectancy.

Growing old

By 2050, studies predict that there will be **1.56 billion** people over the age of **65**, making up about **17 per cent** of the world's population.

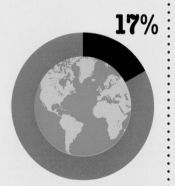

17%

1.56 billion

Aging Americans

By 2050, the number of people over 65 in the USA will **more than double**. It is predicted that the number of people aged **over 100** will soar from 72,000 to 834,000.

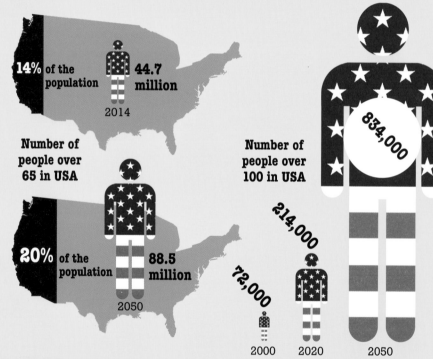

14% of the population   **44.7 million**
2014

Number of people over 65 in USA

20% of the population   **88.5 million**
2050

Number of people over 100 in USA

834,000

214,000

72,000

2000   2020   2050

Oldest person who's ever lived

Jeanne Louise Calment from France lived for 122 years 164 days, from 21 February 1875 to 4 August 1997.

Born 21 February 1875

1876: Alexander Graham Bell invents the telephone.

1903: The Wright Brothers make the first powered flight at Kitty Hawk, North Carollina, USA.

1928: The first transatlantic television signal is sent between London and New York.

1875   1885   1895   1905   1915   1925

Lowest life expectancy

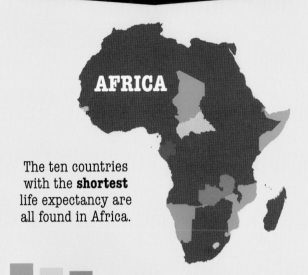

AFRICA

The ten countries with the **shortest** life expectancy are all found in Africa.

- Mozambique – 52.94 years
- Lesotho – 52.86 years
- Zambia – 52.15 years
- Gabon – 52.04 years
- Somalia – 51.96 years
- Central African Republic – 51.81 years
- Namibia – 51.62 years
- Swaziland – 51.05 years
- Guinea-Bissau – 50.23 years
- Chad – 49.81 years

PLACES WHERE PEOPLE LIVE THE LONGEST
(LIFE EXPECTANCY – YEARS)

1. **Monaco – 89.52**
2. Japan – 84.74
3. **Singapore – 84.68**
4. Macau – 84.51
5. **San Marino – 83.24**
6. Iceland – 82.97
7. **Hong Kong – 82.86**
8. Andorra – 82.72
9. **Switzerland – 82.50**
10. Guernsey – 82.47

A Swiss man born in 1900 had a life expectancy of **51**. One born in 2000 can expect to live to **85**. By 2050, some studies show that **2.2 million** Swiss, nearly **30 per cent**, will be older than 65.

1900   2000

Aging Swiss

1010 0101

1938: The world's first freely programmable computer, the Z1, is built by Konrad Zuse.

1961: Yuri Gagarin becomes the first person to orbit Earth.

1969: Apollo 11 mission lands the first people on the Moon.

1978: Louise Brown, the world's first test tube baby, is born.

Dies 4 August 1997

1945   1955   1965   1975   1985   1995

MANY HAPPY RETURNS

<── • ──>

quahog dies 2006

2000

1945 – World War II ends

1900

1876 – Alexander Graham Bell invents the telephone

1800

1776 – Declaration of Independence creates the USA

1700

1616 – William Shakespeare dies

1600

1506 – Leonardo da Vinci paints the *Mona Lisa*

1500

quahog born 1499

Record breaker

The longest-living creature was an ocean quahog (a type of mussel) that was 507 years old when it was killed accidentally by scientists in 2006. It was born in 1499.

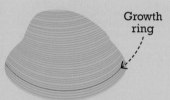

Growth ring

Scientists can tell the age of a quahog by counting the growth rings in the creature's shell – just like the growth rings in a tree trunk.

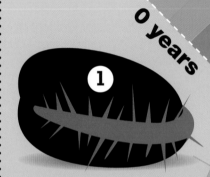

50 years

0 years

1

400 years

350 years

LONGEST LIVING ANIMALS

1. **Ocean quahog – 500 years**
2. Bowhead whale – 211 years
3. **Rougheye rockfish – 205 years**
4. Red sea urchin – 200 years
5. **Galapagos tortoise – 177 years**
6. Shortraker rockfish – 157 years
=7. **Lake sturgeon – 152 years**
=7. Aldabara giant tortoise – 152 years
9. **Orange roughy – 149 years**
10. Warty oreo – 140 years

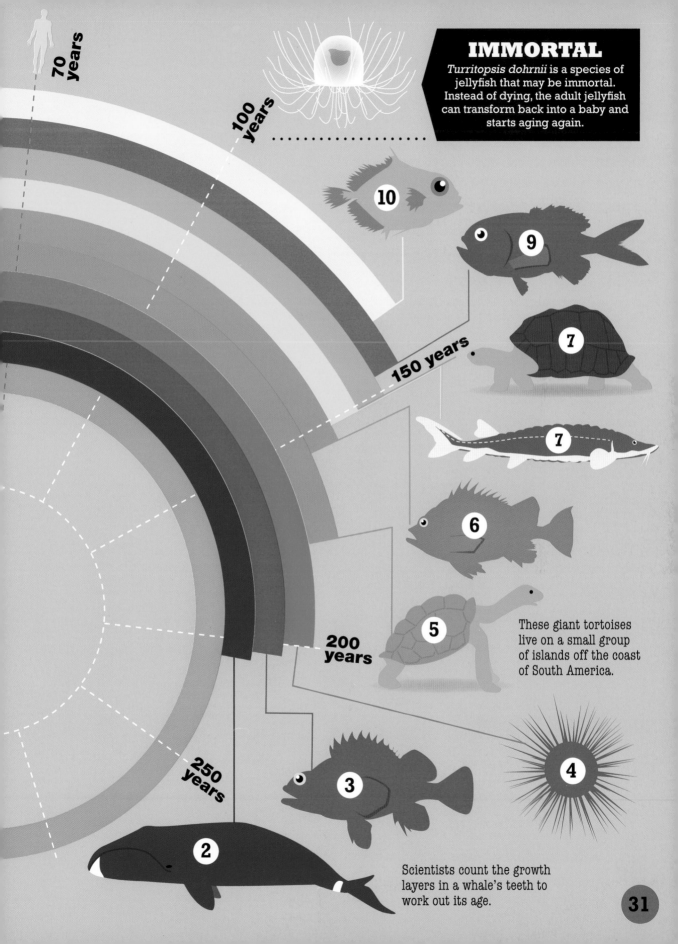

70 years

100 years

IMMORTAL

Turritopsis dohrnii is a species of jellyfish that may be immortal. Instead of dying, the adult jellyfish can transform back into a baby and starts aging again.

10

9

150 years

7

7

6

200 years

5

These giant tortoises live on a small group of islands off the coast of South America.

4

250 years

3

2

Scientists count the growth layers in a whale's teeth to work out its age.

31

BODY
EXTREMES

Growing the longest body parts can take decades of dedicated care and attention. Other body part records, however, come a little more naturally.

1 Longest hair

Xie Qiuping of China has been growing her hair for more than 40 years. It is now nearly three times as long as a bed.

5.627 m

2 Longest nails

Lee Redmond of the USA spent nearly 30 years growing and looking after her nails.

8.65 m (total length)

3 Longest nose

When measured from the bridge of the nose to its tip, Mehmet Ozyurek of Turkey has the longest nose of any living person.

8.8 cm

Life size!

4 Longest moustache

Ram Singh Chauhan of India grew a moustache that was longer than a Volkswagen Beetle.

4.29 m

196 cm

132 cm

5 Longest legs

Svetlana Pankratova from Russia holds the record for the world's longest legs. They make up more than two-thirds of her total height!

132 cm

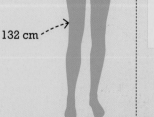

6

Most fingers and toes

Akshat Saxena from India was born with a condition called polydactylism – he had more fingers and toes than normal.

14 fingers (7 on each hand)
20 toes

1.8-m-tall man

7 Largest hands

Robert Wadlow of the USA had hands that measured 32.3 cm from the wrist to the tip of the middle finger.

32.3 cm

8 Largest feet

He also had the largest feet ever measured. They were 47 cm long!

US size 37AA or UK size 36

Robert Waldow's shoe size

Average men's shoe size (US size 10 or UK size 9)

9 Tallest person

In fact, Robert Wadlow holds the record as the tallest person who has ever lived.

2.72 m

10 Shortest person

In contrast, Chandra Bahadur Dangi from Nepal is the shortest living person and is only one-fifth of Wadlow's height.

54.6 cm

KILLER CREATURES

The animals shown here are some of the deadliest on the planet and kill the most people every year. Some are ferocious predators, while others carry killer diseases.

In North America, more people are killed by deer (130 per year) than by grizzly bears (about 2.5 fatal attacks per year on average). Deer are involved in more than 1.5 million car crashes each year.

130 **VS** 2.5

Surprisingly deadly

= 5,000 deaths per year

Dog (rabies)
The greatest risk from dogs is an infected bite. Rabies has a survival rate of less than 10 per cent.

3

25,000

Asian cobra
The powerful venom delivered in this snake's bite can cause heart failure and suffocation.

2

50,000

Tsetse fly (sleeping sickness)
This blood-sucking fly carries a parasite which causes the deadly sleeping sickness.

=4

10,000

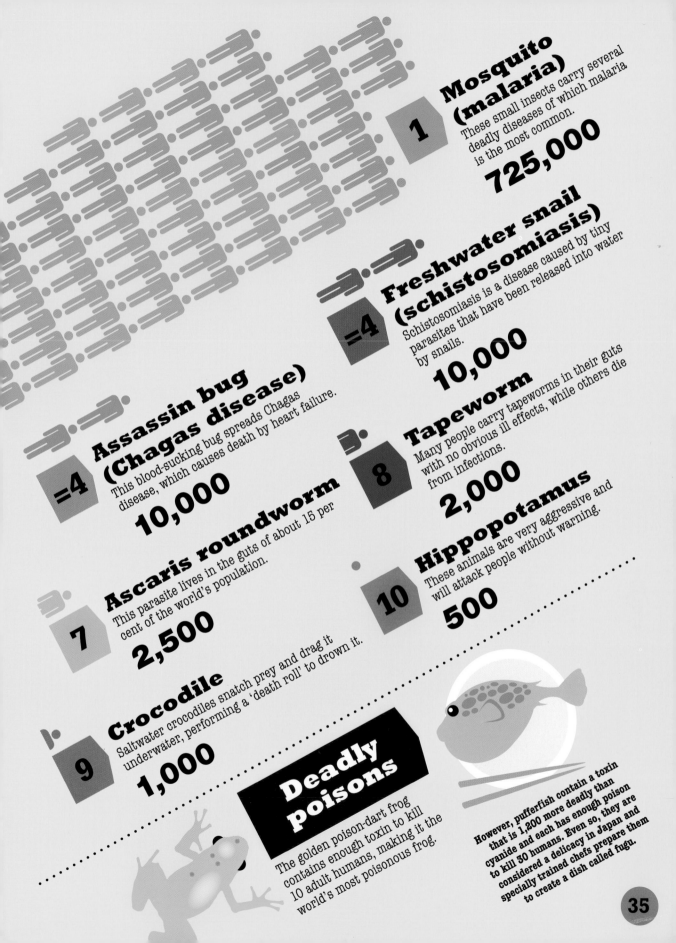

Mosquito (malaria)

1

These small insects carry several deadly diseases of which malaria is the most common.

725,000

Freshwater snail (schistosomiasis)

=4

Schistosomiasis is a disease caused by tiny parasites that have been released into water by snails.

10,000

Assassin bug (Chagas disease)

=4

This blood-sucking bug spreads Chagas disease, which causes death by heart failure.

10,000

Tapeworm

8

Many people carry tapeworms in their guts with no obvious ill effects, while others die from infections.

2,000

Ascaris roundworm

7

This parasite lives in the guts of about 15 per cent of the world's population.

2,500

Hippopotamus

10

These animals are very aggressive and will attack people without warning.

500

Crocodile

9

Saltwater crocodiles snatch prey and drag it underwater, performing a 'death roll' to drown it.

1,000

Deadly poisons

The golden poison-dart frog contains enough toxin to kill 10 adult humans, making it the world's most poisonous frog.

However, pufferfish contain a toxin that is 1,200 more deadly than cyanide and each has enough poison to kill 30 humans. Even so, they are considered a delicacy in Japan and specially trained chefs prepare them to create a dish called fugu.

WORLD OF GIANTS

Giant creatures have many advantages over small ones. Being big and strong makes it easier to defeat other animals, while being tall makes it easier to reach out-of-the-way food. Large animals are also better insulated against extreme heat and cold.

The figure by each human silhouette represents the number of adult humans each animal weighs.

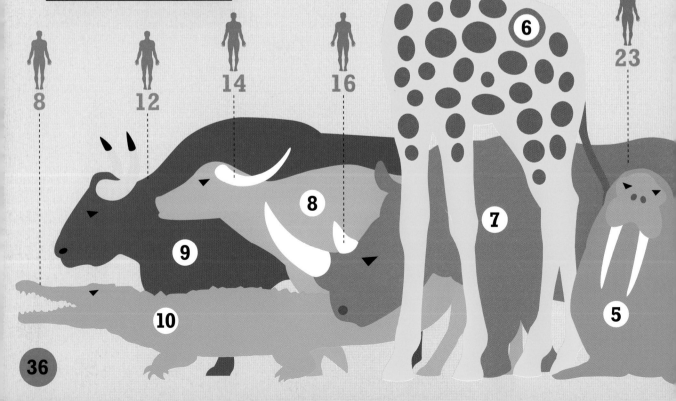

18

6

8

12

14

16

23

9

8

7

10

5

Biggest bony fish

Fish have skeletons that are either made from bone, or from bendy cartilage. The biggest fish with a skeleton made from bone is the mola mola, which is 3.3 m across and weighs 1,900 kg.

HEAVIEST LAND ANIMALS

1. **African elephant – 5.25 tonnes**
2. Asian elephant – 3.5 tonnes
3. **White rhinoceros – 2.5 tonnes**
4. Hippopotamus – 2.3 tonnes
5. **Walrus – 1.6 tonnes**
6. Giraffe – 1.25 tonnes
7. **Black rhinoceros – 1.15 tonnes**
8. Wild Asian water buffalo – 0.98 tonnes
9. **Gaur – 0.85 tonnes**
10. Saltwater crocodile – 0.6 tonnes

Humans weigh 70 kg (0.07 tonnes) on average, but the heaviest person was Joe Brower Minnoch who weighed more than 635 kg (0.635 tonnes).

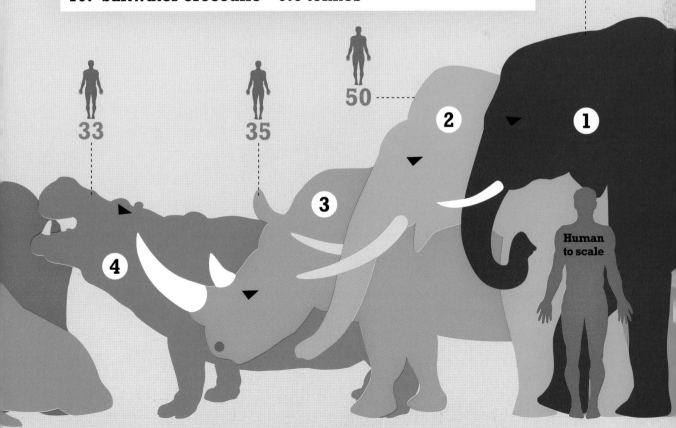

33

35

50

75

2

1

3

4

Human to scale

BIG BUGS

4

Insects are some of the most successful forms of life on Earth and make up about half of all species on the planet. They all have a tough outer skeleton and six jointed legs.

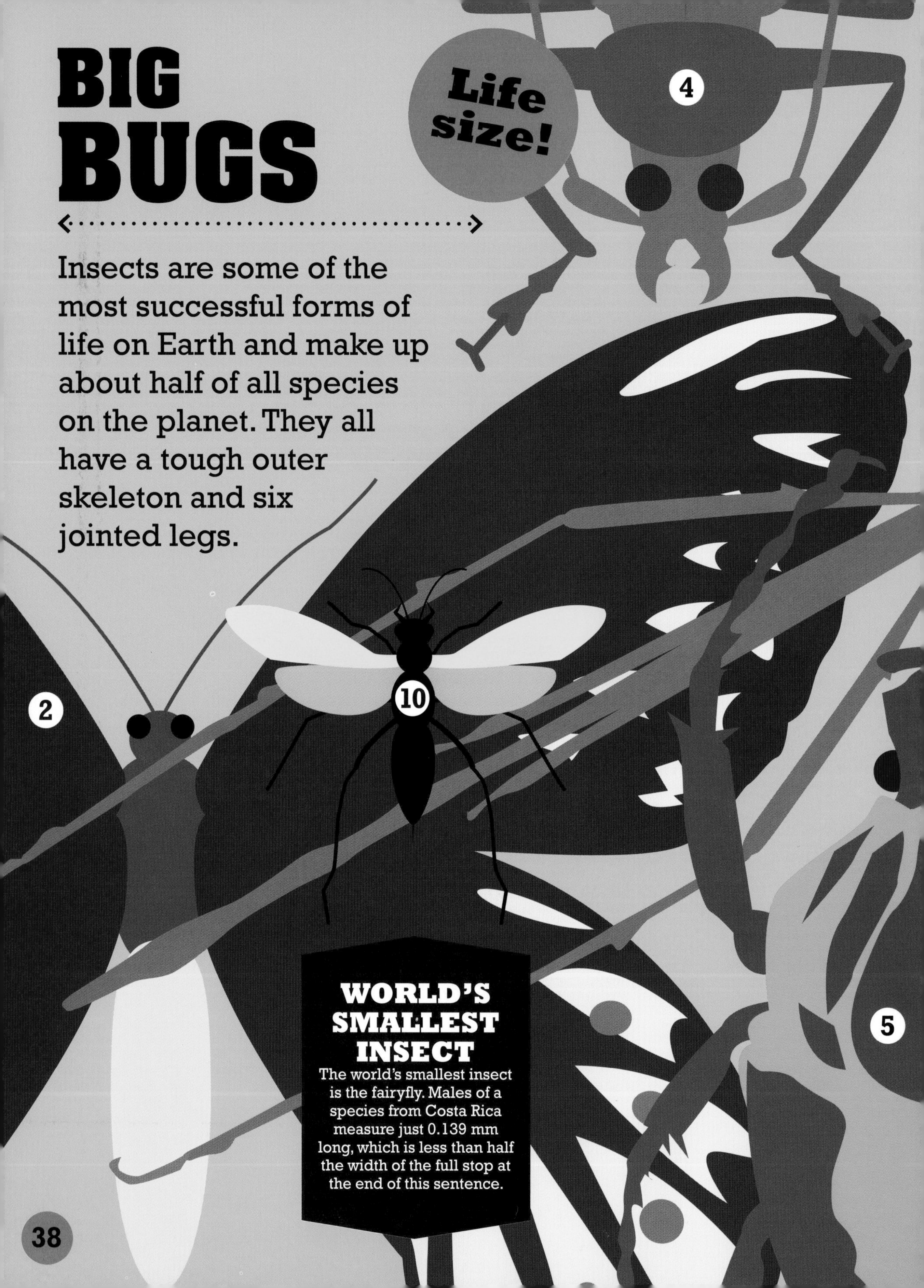

2

10

5

WORLD'S SMALLEST INSECT

The world's smallest insect is the fairyfly. Males of a species from Costa Rica measure just 0.139 mm long, which is less than half the width of the full stop at the end of this sentence.

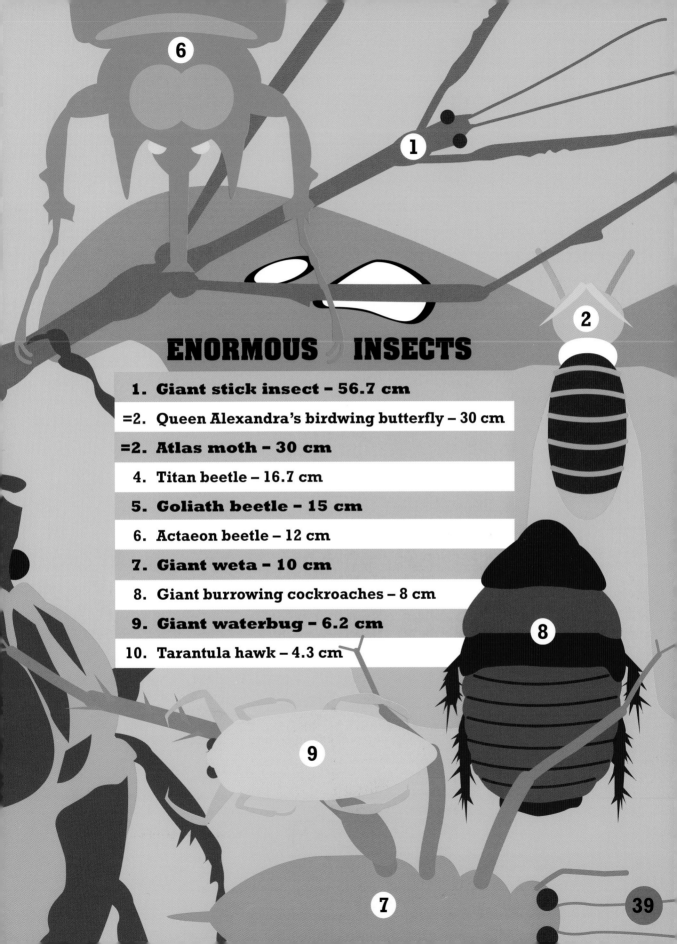

ENORMOUS INSECTS

1. **Giant stick insect – 56.7 cm**
=2. **Queen Alexandra's birdwing butterfly – 30 cm**
=2. **Atlas moth – 30 cm**
4. **Titan beetle – 16.7 cm**
5. **Goliath beetle – 15 cm**
6. **Actaeon beetle – 12 cm**
7. **Giant weta – 10 cm**
8. **Giant burrowing cockroaches – 8 cm**
9. **Giant waterbug – 6.2 cm**
10. **Tarantula hawk – 4.3 cm**

THE BIG SLEEP

Some animals spend part of the year in a long sleep-like period called hibernation, when food and water are in short supply and the conditions are harsh. These pages list some of the longest hibernators.

Fat-tailed dwarf lemur

During hibernation, these lemurs lose 50 per cent of their weight.

7 months

Alpine marmot

During hibernation, this mammal's heart rate slows from 120 beats per minute (bpm) to just 4 bpm.

8 months

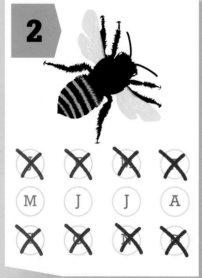

Bumblebee (queen)

The queen bee is the only one that sleeps through the winter – all the other bees die. After the winter, the queen wakes up and starts to lay eggs to re-form the hive.

6–8 months

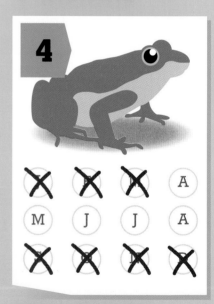

Wood frog

These amphibians produce a natural 'anti-freeze' to protect themselves through the cold winter months.

7 months

Summer sleep

While some animals hibernate during cold, winter months, other creatures enter a similar state when conditions are very warm and dry. This condition is called aestivation and it stops animals

Arctic ground squirrel

These mammals shelter in small burrows dug into the tundra.

6 months

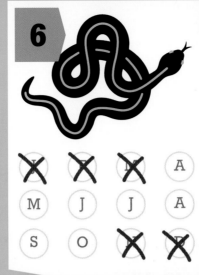

Garter snake

These snakes hibernate in huge groups to keep each other warm.

5 months

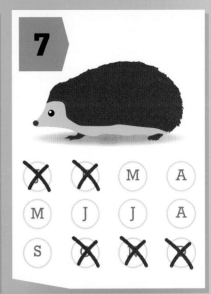

Hedgehog

If the weather gets too cold during hibernation, a hedgehog wakes up and moves to a warmer place.

4–5 months

Common poorwill

This is the only known bird species to hibernate through the winter.

3–4 months

Black bear

For more than 100 days during hibernation, bears will not eat, drink, urinate or defecate.

3–4 months

Big brown bat

During hibernation, this bat's heart rate will drop from 1,000 bpm to just 25 bpm.

2 months

from drying out. Creatures that do this include snails, beetles, tortoises and frogs.

MOVING ANIMALS

384,400 km

Many animals travel thousands of kilometres every year looking for places to eat, to mate and to give birth and raise young. This movement is called migration.

Record flier

During its lifetime, an individual Arctic tern will fly more than 800,000 km – that's more than twice the distance between Earth and the Moon.

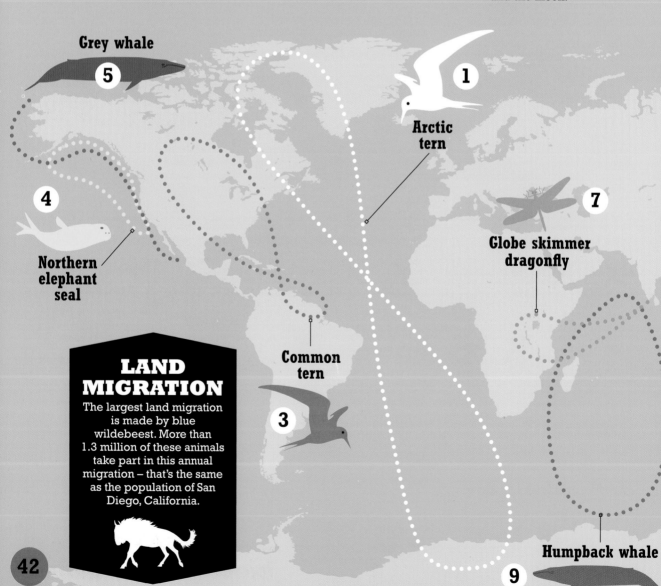

Grey whale

5

1

Arctic tern

7

Globe skimmer dragonfly

4

Northern elephant seal

LAND MIGRATION

The largest land migration is made by blue wildebeest. More than 1.3 million of these animals take part in this annual migration – that's the same as the population of San Diego, California.

Common tern

3

Humpback whale

9

LONGEST ANNUAL MIGRATIONS

1. **Arctic tern – 70,000 km**
2. **Sooty shearwater – 64,000 km**
3. **Common tern – 26,000 km**
4. **Northern elephant seal – 21,000 km**
5. **Grey whale – 20,000 km**
6. **Leatherback turtle – 19,300 km**
7. **Globe skimmer dragonfly – 15,000 km**
8. **Bar-tailed godwit – 11,000 km**
9. **Humpback whale – 8,300 km**
10. **Tuna – 7,700 km**

The Arctic tern follows a long figure-of-eight shape between the Arctic and Antarctic. This makes the journey more than four times the distance a direct route would be.

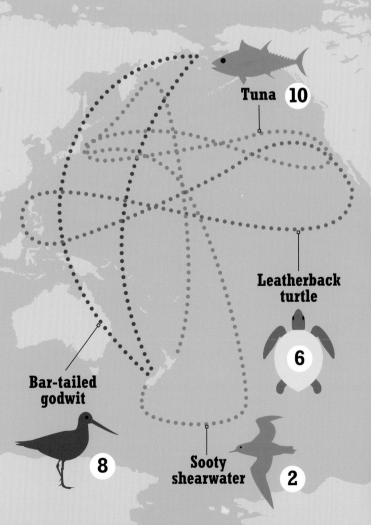

Tuna **10**

Leatherback turtle **6**

Bar-tailed godwit **8**

Sooty shearwater **2**

Caribou

One of the longest migrations on land is made by caribou. They travel about 5,000 km every year – that's the same as the distance from Paris to Beijing.

x44

To prepare for its migration, a caribou will eat about 5 kg of food every day during the summer, which is the same weight as 44 burgers!

Every day, billions of tiny creatures called zooplankton migrate up towards the ocean surface and down again in a movement called vertical migration.

Up and down

LIFE ON EARTH

<‹ ·· ›>

Earth is the only place in the Solar System where life has been found (so far). It is the perfect distance from the Sun to be the right temperature for liquid water, which is vital for life, to exist.

1

The **forested area** of Russia is about the same size as the **entire country** of Brazil.

2

3

4

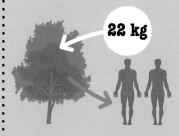
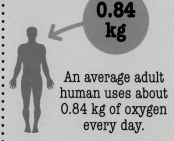

COUNTRIES WITH THE LARGEST COMBINED FOREST AREA

1. **Russia – 8.5 million sq km**
2. Brazil – 5.4 million sq km
3. **Canada – 2.4 million sq km**
4. USA – 2.3 million sq km
5. **China – 1.6 million sq km**
6. Australia – 1.5 million sq km
7. **Dem Rep of Congo – 1.4 million sq km**
8. Indonesia – 1 million sq km
9. **Angola – 698,000 sq km**
10. Peru – 652,000 sq km

Biomass facts

The combined mass of living things is called biomass. These figures show the creatures with some of the greatest biomass.

Humans 350 million tonnes
Seven billion people weighing an average of 50 kg each.

Termites 445 million tonnes
A single termite nest can be home to millions of individual termites.

Atlantic Krill 379 million tonnes
Trillions of these tiny creatures swarm together providing food for other marine animals.

Cows 650 million tonnes
There are only 1.3 billion cows in the world, but they weigh 500 kg each, making their total biomass nearly twice that of humans.

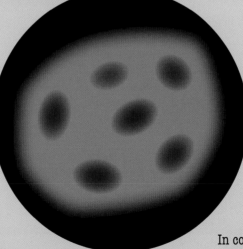

Cyanobacteria 1 billion tonnes
Some of the smallest living things on the planet, make up the greatest amount of biomass.

Blue Whales 0.5 million tonnes
In contrast, the total biomass of the largest animal to have ever lived is just 0.5 million tonnes.

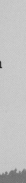

5   6   7   8   9   10

CRACKED SURFACE

<------------------------------------->

The surface of Earth is cracked like the shell of an egg into various, uneven and jagged tectonic plates. These move around slowly, bashing into each other and creating shattering earthquakes, spouting volcanoes and towering mountains.

What's inside a volcano

A volcano is an opening in the crust where molten rock, ash, steam and gases escape from the planet's interior.

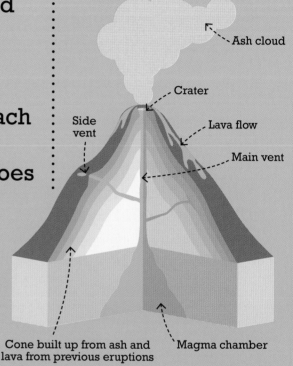

- Ash cloud
- Crater
- Side vent
- Lava flow
- Main vent
- Cone built up from ash and lava from previous eruptions
- Magma chamber

Most active volcano

The most active volcano on the planet is Kilauea in Hawaii. It has been erupting continuously since 1983 and lava erupts from it at a rate of 5 cubic metres every second.

8 mins 20 sec

That's fast enough to fill an Olympic swimming pool in ...

Lava reaches 1,250°C – hot enough to melt gold.

Pyroclastic flows are clouds of scorching rock and gas that pour out of a volcano. They typically move at speeds of 80 km/h, but the fastest can travel at **480 km/h**, which is **1.5 times faster** than a Formula One car.

How mountains are formed

Everest is the tallest mountain on Earth and is **8,848 m** high. It was created by two tectonic plates crashing into each other, forming the towering **Himalayas**.

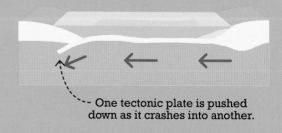

One tectonic plate is pushed down as it crashes into another.

90%
of volcanoes are found around the Pacific Ring of Fire.

Volcanoes can send an ash cloud up to an altitude of 30 km.

That's 3.5 times the height of Everest.

LARGEST TECTONIC PLATES

1. Pacific – 103,300,000 sq km
2. North America – 75,900,000 sq km
3. Eurasia – 67,800,000 sq km
4. Africa – 61,300,000 sq km
5. Antarctica – 60,900,000 sq km
6. Australia – 47,000,000 sq km
7. South America 43,600,000 sq km
8. Somalia – 16,700,000 sq km
9. Nazca – 15,600,000 sq km
10. India – 11,900,000 sq km

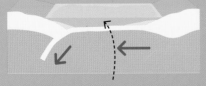

As the plates move together, the rock between them starts to clump up.

Rock is pushed up between the plates, creating mountains.

Growing Himalayas

The Himalayas are currently growing at a rate of about 1 cm per year.

DRY PLANET

<‹ · ›>

Deserts are the driest places on the planet, receiving less than 25 cm of precipitation a year. They cover about one-third of the land and range in habitat from the scorching wastes of the Sahara in Africa to the frozen realm of Antarctica.

Ice desert

Antarctica is the largest desert in the world (bigger than the continental USA). It is actually covered with water, but that is all **frozen**.

The **average thickness** of the ice is more than 1.6 km. That's twice the height of the **Burj Khalifa**, the world's tallest building (see pages 56–7).

Atacama Desert

The **Atacama Desert** in Chile is a rain shadow desert and the driest place on the planet. Its average rainfall is just 0.1 mm per year – that's just **1 cm of rain every 100 years.**

If the ice caps melted the sea level would rise **60 m** ...

Flooded

... and the world's coastlines would look like this.

The **hottest** and **coldest** temperatures recorded on Earth were both measured in **deserts**.

−89.2°C	−12.3°C	−18°C	0°C	15°C	37°C	56.7°C
Vostok Station, Antarctica	Highest temperature recorded at the South Pole	Optimum temperature for a freezer	Freezing point of water	Average temperature of Earth	Body temperature	Furnace Creek, Death Valley, California

 Lowest

✶ Highest

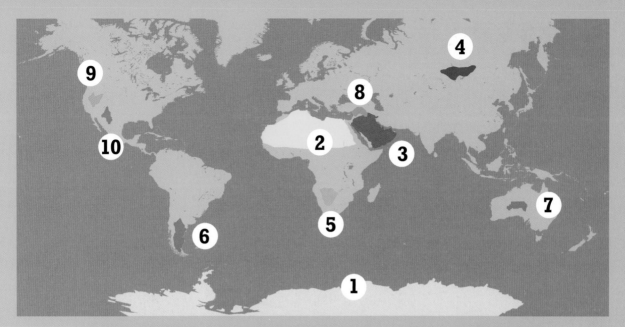

LARGEST DESERTS IN THE WORLD

1. **Antarctica – 14.2 million sq km**

2. Sahara – 8.6 million sq km

3. **Arabian Desert – 2.3 million sq km**

4. Gobi Desert – 1.3 million sq km

5. **Kalahari Desert – 930,000 sq km**

6. Patagonian Desert – 673,000 sq km

7. **Great Victoria Desert – 647,000 sq km**

8. Syrian desert – 518,000 sq km

9. **Great Basin Desert – 492,000 sq km**

10. Chihuahuan Desert – 282,000 sq km

How a rain shadow desert forms

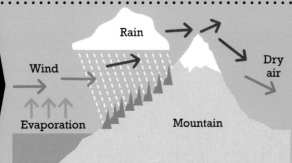

Rain

Wind

Evaporation

Dry air

Mountain

Water vapour is picked up from the ocean to create moist air. This air is pushed up by a mountain range, where the water falls as rain. This leaves **dry air** to pass over to the other side of the mountains, creating the very dry conditions that form rain shadow deserts.

ANIMALS UNDER THREAT

Changes in the environment, such as global warming and habitat loss, can threaten an animal's existence. If that change is great enough, it can push whole species to the brink of extinction.

Habitat loss

By 2100, it is predicted that annual sea ice will have declined by 10–50 per cent and summer sea ice will have decreased by 50–100 per cent. This will affect the habitat of polar bears and reduce their numbers by 30 per cent.

Current population 25,000

Projected population 17,500

2100

2015

50%

In the last 100 years, about half of all coral reefs...

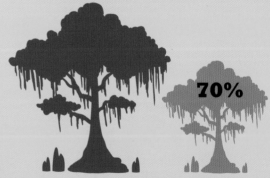

70%

... and nearly one-third of mangrove forests have been lost.

MOST ENDANGERED ANIMALS (NUMBER LEFT)

=1. **Ivory-billed woodpecker – may be extinct**

=1. **Saola – may be extinct**

3. **Northern sportive lemur – 18**

4. **Amur leopard – 20**

5. **Javan rhinoceros – 40**

6. **North Pacific Right Whale – 50**

7. **White-headed langur – < 70**

8. **Vaquita – 100–300**

9. **Cross river gorilla – 200–300**

10. **Sumatran tiger – 441–679**

Some scientists believe that animal species are becoming extinct faster than new species are being discovered.

Climate change

The UN Climate Panel states that an increase in the average global temperature of just 1°C will lead to an increasing risk of extinction for 30 per cent of species on Earth.

13°C (average temperature)

1°C increase

30 per cent

Three species per hour

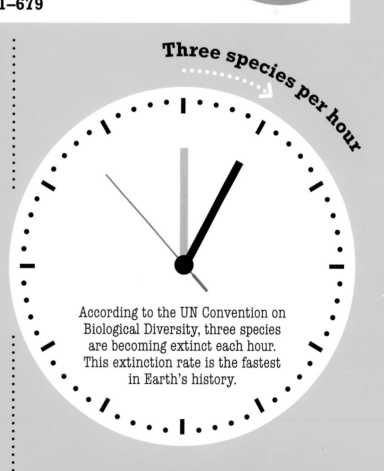

According to the UN Convention on Biological Diversity, three species are becoming extinct each hour. This extinction rate is the fastest in Earth's history.

Ticking clock

PET PLANET

People have lived with animals for thousands of years – either for food and clothing, for working, to hunt, or just for good company. Over the years, we have created different breeds to produce animals with varying characteristics.

Smallest dog

The smallest dog ever was a dwarf Yorkshire terrier called Sylvia – she stood 6.3 cm at the shoulder and was just 9.5 cm from nose to tail.

Life size!

The farthest distance a lost pet dog has walked to find his way home is **3,218 km.** Jimpa, a Labrador/boxer cross walked from a farm at Nyabing, Western Australia, to Pimpinio, Victoria, taking **14 months** to do so.

AUSTRALIA

Nyabing

Pimpinio

The UK has a pet fish population of up to 50 million. Half of these are kept in tanks, while the other half are kept in outdoor ponds.

More than **60 per cent** of Australians have a pet, more than any other nationality.

60%

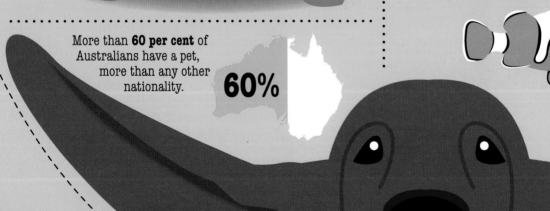

34.3 cm

COUNTRIES WITH THE MOST PET CATS

1. **USA – 76,430,000**
2. China – 53,100,000
3. Russia – 12,700,000
4. Brazil – **12,466,000**
5. France – 9,600,000
6. Italy – 9,400,000
=7. UK – 7,700,000
=7. Germany – 7,700,000
9. Ukraine – 7,350,000
10. Japan – 7,300,000

With more than 76 million cats, the USA has one cat for every four people

Largest litter

19

The largest litter by a domestic cat is **19**. In comparison, the average litter size is just **4–6**.

Longest ears

Harbor the Coonhound holds the record for the longest dog ears ever. His right ear measured **34.3 cm** from head to tip and his left ear measured **31.1 cm**.

31.1 cm

1
2
3
4
5
6
=7
=7
9
10

BUILDING FOR ANIMALS

Animals need lots of space to live in – some zoos cover enormous areas! They also need to meet each animal's specific needs and be super-tough to withstand tonnes of water and strong beasts.

Hengoin Ocean Kingdom

The aquarium at the Hengoin Ocean Kingdom holds enough water to fill nearly 20 Olympic swimming pools.

1

2

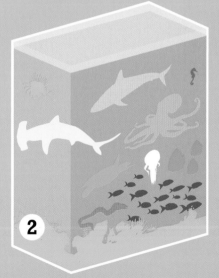

Big bird park

Located in Kuala Lumpur, Malaysia, the KL Bird Park is the largest free flight aviary in the world. It covers 8.5 hectares and is home to 3,000 birds from 200 species.

LARGEST AQUARIUMS (LITRES)

1. **Hengoin Ocean Kingdom (China) – 48.72 million**

2. Georgia Aquarium (USA) – 23.84 million

3. **Dubai Mall Aquarium (Dubai) – 9.99 million**

4. Okinawa Churaumi Aquarium (Japan) – 7.5 million

5. **L'Oceanografic (Spain) – 7 million**

6. Turkuazoo (Turkey) – 5 million

7. **Monterrey Bay Aquarium (USA) – 4.54 million**

=8. uShaka Marine World (South Africa) – < 3.8 million

=8. **Shanghai Ocean Aquarium (China) – < 3.8 million**

=8. Aquarium of Genoa (Italy) – < 3.8 million

The penguin pool at London Zoo covers 1,200 sq metres and holds 450,000 litres. That's enough to fill more than 5,500 baths and give you a bath every day for the next 15 years!

x 5,500

Penguin pool

3

4

5

6

7

8

9

10

One wall of the Dubai Mall Aquarium is made from an enormous panel of transparent acrylic – the largest in the world. It measures 32.88 m by 8.3 m, making it bigger than a tennis court.

Toronto zoo

Toronto Zoo is one of the largest zoos in the world. It has over 5,000 animals from 500 different species.

The zoo has 10 km of walking trails (enough to go around an athletics track 25 times) and covers 287 hectares – about the same size as Central Park in Manhattan, New York City, USA.

- - Central Park

Manhattan

TALLER AND TALLER ········>

Advances in technology over the last 100 years have seen the world's tallest buildings nearly quadruple in size.

The biggest skyscrapers are now nearly a kilometre high and really do have their heads in the clouds!

These graphics show

the buildings that have held the title of the world's tallest building over the last 100 years. They are compared to the height of a giraffe.

Moving Tower

Changes in temperature throughout the year cause the Eiffel Tower to expand and contract by as much as 18 cm. Powerful winds also push the top of the tower, causing it to sway by 7 cm.

7 cm

At just 301 m tall, the Eiffel Tower in Paris is less than half the height of the Burj Khalifa.

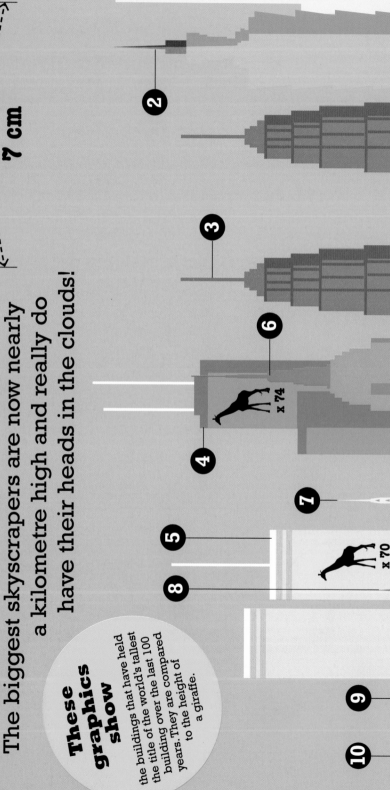

x 74

x 70

1

2

3

4

5

6

7

8

9

10

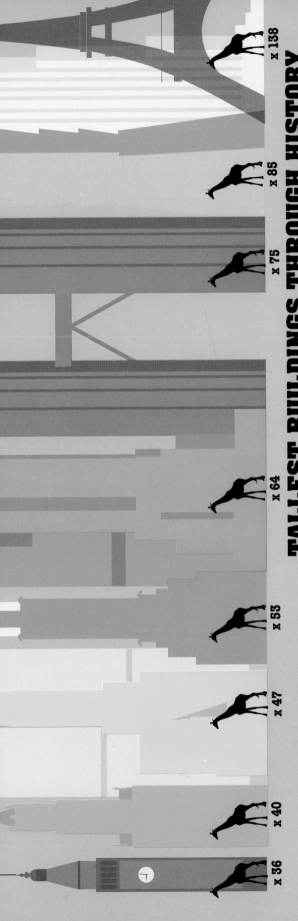

x 138

x 85

x 75

x 64

x 53

x 47

x 40

x 36

TALLEST BUILDINGS THROUGH HISTORY

1. **Burj Khalifa, Dubai (since 2010) – 828 m**

2. **Taipei 101, Taiwan (2004–2007) – 509 m**

3. **Petronas Towers, Malaysia (1998–2004) – 452 m**

4. **Willis Tower, USA (1974–1998) – 442 m**

5. **World Trade Center, USA (1972–1974) – 417 m**

6. **Empire State Building, USA (1931–1972) – 381 m**

7. **Chrysler Building, USA (1930–1931) – 319 m**

8. **The Trump Building, USA (1930) – 283 m**

9. **Woolworth Building, USA (1913–1930) – 241 m**

10. **Metropolitan Life Building, USA (1909–1913) – 213 m**

Empire State Building

This skyscraper is struck by lightning on average 23 times a year.

The observatory on the 102nd floor was originally designed to be a check-in area for airships that would moor to the top.

SPEND, SPEND, SPEND

Shopping malls are enormous buildings that can contain hundreds of shops. Many of the largest also feature theme parks, restaurants and cinemas to keep shoppers happy and spending their money.

Mega mall

The Dubai Mall is the largest mall in the world in terms of total area, but only the 14th largest in terms of leasable area (the area taken up by shops).

shops
1,200

200 restaurants

It has the world's largest sweet shop – Candylicious. This covers 930 sq m, which is about **1.5 football pitches.**

It has 80 million visitors every year ...

Germany: population 80,996,000

... more than any other place on Earth and close to the total population of Germany.

Its shops can take more than £3 billion in a year ...

£1,400

... that's enough to give every person living in Dubai £1,400 per year.

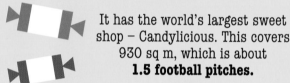
Total area = 1,124,000 sq m
Leasable area = 350,000 sq m

Vatican City 440,000 sq m

Supermarkets

The first supermarket in the US was King Kullen Supermarket, which opened on Jamaica Avenue, New York City, in August 1930.

It covered just 560 sq m (a basketball court is 420 sq m).

In contrast, Jungle Jim's International Market, in Ohio, USA, covers more than 18,500 sq m – more than 30 times the area of King Kullen Supermarket and three times the area of the White House.

Walmart is one of the biggest supermarket chains in the world.

It has ...

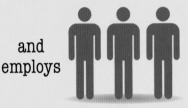

more than 11,000 stores in **28 countries** and employs **2.3 million staff**

LARGEST SHOPPING MALLS (LEASABLE AREA)

1. **New South China Mall (Dongguan, China)**	**600,153 sq m**
2. Golden Resources Mall (Beijing, China)	557,419 sq m
3. **SM Megamall (Mandaluyong, Philippines)**	**506,435 sq m**
4. SM City North EDSA (Quezon City, Philippines)	482,878 sq m
5. **1 Utama (Petaling Jaya, Selangor, Malaysia)**	**465,000 sq m**
6. Persian Gulf Complex (Shiraz, Iran)	450,000 sq m
7. **Central World (Bangkok, Thailand)**	**429,500 sq m**
8. Isfahan City Center (Isfahan, Iran)	425,000 sq m
=9. **Mid Valley Megamall (Kuala Lumpur, Malaysia)**	**420,000 sq m**
=9. Cevahir Mall (Istanbul, Turkey)	420,000 sq m

59

THAT'S RICH!

These people are the richest on the planet. They have accumulated huge amounts of wealth in industries such as computer software, airlines, telecommunications and investments.

Where do the billionaires live?

This map shows the **distribution** of the world's billionaires, with most living in **Europe and Russia** and the fewest found in **Australasia**.

Total number of billionaires **1,682**

North America
441

26%

6%

Latin America
94

RICHEST PEOPLE

1. **Bill Gates (USA) – US$75 bn**
2. **Amancio Ortega (Spain) – US$67 bn**
3. **Warren Buffett (USA) – US$60.8 bn**
4. **Carlos Sim Helu (Mexico) – US$50 bn**
5. **Jeff Bezos (USA) – US$45.2 bn**
6. **Mark Zuckerberg (USA) – US$44.6 bn**
7. **Larry Ellison (USA) – US$43.6 bn**
8. **Michael Bloomberg (USA) – US$40 bn**
=9. **Charles Koch (USA) – US$39.6 bn**
=9. **David Koch (USA) – US$39.6 bn**

Bill Gates, the world's richest person, has given away more than US$30 billion to charitable causes since 2000, through the Bill and Melinda Gates Foundation.

Richest city

The city with the most billionaires is Moscow. It has ...

... **84 billionaires** with a combined wealth of **US$366 bn.**

This is enough wealth to purchase nearly **750,000 gold bullion bars**

It is also more than the Gross Domestic Product (annual earnings) of the country of South Africa.

Europe and Russia
505
30%

Moscow

29%

Asia
488

1.5%

Africa
25

Middle East
108

6.5%

Australasia
21

1%

Where can money take you?

Changed into quarters (25-cent coins), this money would create a stack of coins **44.8 million km tall.** That's long enough to stretch nearly **1,120 times around the globe** or more than ...

The total combined wealth of the world's billionaires comes to **US$6.4 trillion.**

Enough to give everyone on the planet **more than US$900.**

... 58 times to the Moon and back.

NO EXPENSE SPARED

Welcome to the most expensive buildings on the planet! They offer bespoke office services, amazing hotel accommodation and the height of private luxury.

1 2 3 4 5 6 7 8 9 10

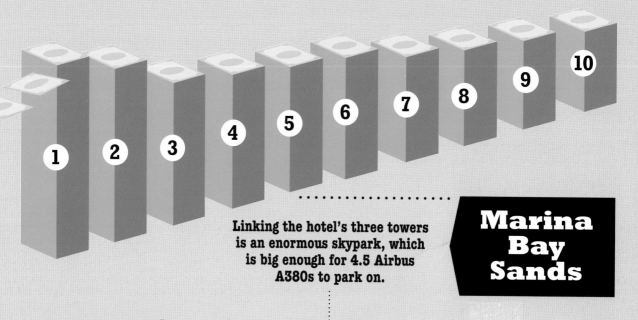

Linking the hotel's three towers is an enormous skypark, which is big enough for 4.5 Airbus A380s to park on.

Marina Bay Sands

The hotel also features a swimming pool that is **150 m long**, a shopping mall, a museum, two theatres and an ice rink.

It was built at a rate of one floor **every four days.**

The largest suites in the Marina Bay Sands measure 629 sq m, about the same area as **two tennis courts.**

The casino inside the hotel has a chandelier which contains 132,000 crystals and weighs 7.1 tonnes – about the weight of three adult hippos!

MOST EXPENSIVE BUILDINGS TO BUILD

1. **Marina Bay Sands (Singapore) – US$6 bn**
2. **Resorts World Sentosa (Singapore) – US$5.38 bn**
3. **Emirates Palace (Abu Dhabi) – US$4.46 bn**
4. **The Cosmopolitan (USA) – US$4.16 bn**
5. **The Shard (UK) – US$3.9 bn**
6. **One World Trade Center (USA) – US$3.8 bn**
7. **Wynn Resort (USA) – US$3.26 bn**
8. **Venetian Macau (Macau) – US$2.97 bn**
9. **City of Dreams (Macau) – US$2.75 bn**
10. **Antilia (India) – US$2.53 bn**

The Prices of these buildings have been adjusted for inflation so that the figures here show the cost if they were all built in 2012.

Living in luxury

The Burj al Arab is a seven-star hotel in Dubai. It has nine restaurants and bars, a health spa, four swimming pools, its own private beach and a helicopter landing pad on the roof.

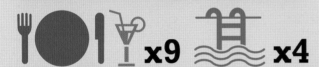

x9 **x4** **x1** **x1**

A Royal Suite here can cost up to £11,435 for a single night!

Most expensive hotel suite

The Royal Penthouse Suite at the Hotel President Wilson, Geneva, Switzerland can cost up to **US$83,200 a night.**

It has 12 bedrooms, 12 bathrooms, a gym, a billiards table and a grand piano.

The suite covers 1,800 sq m – larger than the area of four basketball courts.

Antilia

Antilia is said to be the most expensive private residence in the world. It has **three helipads** and a multi-storey garage with space for **168 cars.**

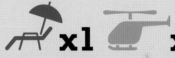

168

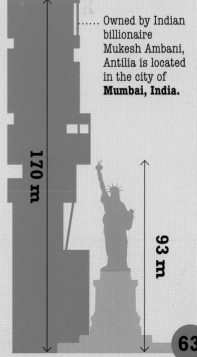

...... Owned by Indian billionaire Mukesh Ambani, Antilia is located in the city of **Mumbai, India.**

170 m

93 m

ON DISPLAY

Millions of people flock to museums around the world every year. These buildings house precious works of art, animal bones and fossils, historical relics and monuments, or amazing inventions. They also have huge storage areas where they keep objects that they cannot display.

1
2
3
4

 = 500,000 visitors

The Smithsonian

The Smithsonian Institution is the world's largest museum complex. It is made up of 19 galleries and museums and houses more than

137 million objects.

If you spent one minute looking at each object for 24 hours a day, it would take more than 260 years to view them all!

 1 min x   x 24 hrs

= 260 years

The British Museum

It has a total area of 92,000 sq m, of which 21,600 sq m is storage space (with a further 9,400 sq m of storage space offsite).

The British Museum can display about 80,000 items at any one time – but that's just 1 per cent of the 8 million items it owns.

MOST POPULAR MUSEUMS

1. **Louvre (Paris) – 9,334,000 visitors a year**
2. National Museum of Natural History (Washington, DC) – 8,000,000
3. **National Museum of China (Beijing) – 7,450,000**
4. National Air and Space Museum (Washington, DC) – 6,970,000
5. **British Museum (London) – 6,701,000**
6. The Metropolitan Museum of Art (NYC) – 6,280,000
7. **National Gallery (London) – 6,031,000**
8. Vatican Museums (Vatican) – 5,459,000
9. **Natural History Museum (London) – 5,250,000**
10. American Museum of Natural History (NYC) – 5,000,000

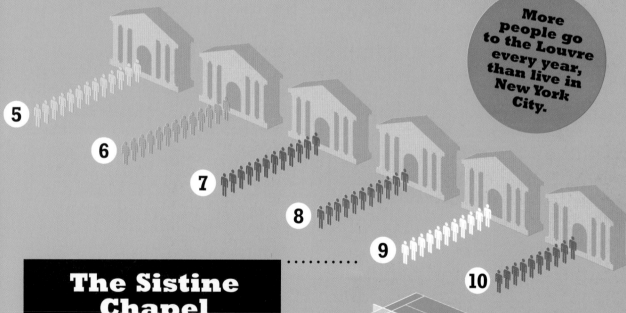

More people go to the Louvre every year, than live in New York City.

The Sistine Chapel

The Vatican in Rome houses a number of museums, including the Sistine Chapel. The ceiling of this features an enormous fresco painted by Michelangelo.

The fresco covers 800 sq m (more than three tennis courts) and took four years to paint (1508–1512).

WORKS OF ART

These paintings were created by some of the best-known artists who ever lived. Although not all achieved success in their lifetimes, their works have gone on to sell for hundreds of millions of dollars.

1

1894–1895

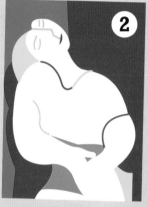

2

1932

Least valuable art collection

The Museum of Bad Art in Boston, USA, holds the record for the least valuable art collection. Its 573 works are worth just US$1,197.35, **or US$2.09 each.**

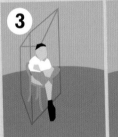

3

1969

4

1948

Vincent Van Gogh produced more than **2,000** works of art, but he only sold **one** while he was alive.

5

1953

6

1907

Oldest art

Made by Neanderthals around **40,000 years ago**, scratches found on a cave wall in Gibraltar may be Europe's oldest art.

MOST EXPENSIVE WORKS OF ART

1. **The Card Players, Paul Cezanne – US$259 million**

2. **La Rêve, Pablo Picasso – US$155 million**

3. **Three studies of Lucian Freud, Francis Bacon – US$142.4 million**

4. **No. 5, 1948, Jackson Pollock – US$140 million**

5. **Woman III, Willem de Kooning – US$137.5 million**

6. **Portrait of Adele Bloch-Bauer I, Gustav Klimt – US$135 million**

7. **The Scream, Edvard Munch – US$119.9 million**

8. **Flag, Jasper Johns – US$110 million**

9. **Nude, Green Leaves and Bust, Pablo Picasso – US$106 million**

10. **Anna's Light, Barnett Newman – US$105.7 million**

7

1893

8

1954–1955

9

1932

10

1968

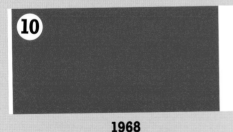

Maree man

This is the largest human art figure ever made. It was carved into the ground in Australia and measured 4.2 km long. It appeared in 1998, and could only be seen from the air. No-one knows who made it or why.

4.2 km

Micro art

Willard Wigan from the UK creates microscopic sculptures. They are so small that they can sit inside the eye of a needle.

Actual size

BEST SELLERS

Every year, billions of books are bought and read either in printed form or on e-readers and tablets. The people on these pages know what makes a good read. Meet the most successful, most prolific and biggest selling authors of all time!

Shakespeare Records

As well as being the world's best-selling author, William Shakespeare is believed to have invented, or introduced, more than **1,700 new words**.

His longest play, *Hamlet*, has 4,042 lines and 29,551 words. The character of Hamlet alone has 1,569 lines.

All of his works were recited over 110 hours in 1987 during the longest ever theatre performance.

Most filmed author

420 films and TV movies

Hamlet 79 movies

Romeo and Juliet 52 movies

Macbeth 36 movies

Largest Book

The largest book in the world is **This is the Prophet Mohamed**, published by the Mshahed International Group, Dubai.

It measures 5 m by 8.06 m, and weighs 1,500 kg.

That's **taller than a giraffe** and weighs more than 20 adults, or **about the weight of a car**.

BESTSELLING AUTHORS OF ALL TIME (ESTIMATED SALES)

1. **William Shakespeare – 2–4.5 billion**
2. **Agatha Christie – 2–4 billion**
=3. **Barbara Cartland – 0.5–1 billion**
=3. **Danielle Steel – 0.5–1 billion**
5. **Harold Robbins – 800 million**
=6. **Georges Simenon – 500–800 million**
=6. **Charles Dickens – 500–800 million**
8. **Sidney Sheldon – 400–600 million**
9. **Enid Blyton – 350–600 million**
10. **Dr Seuss 100–500 million**

The Way to Happiness

by L. Ron Hubbard is the most translated (non-religious) book in the world. It can be read in 70 different languages, including Samoan and Uzbek.

Largest bookstore

The world's largest bookstore is Barnes & Noble in New York City, USA. It covers **14,330 sq m, the size of nearly 2.5 football pitches.**

... and has **20.71 km of shelves.**

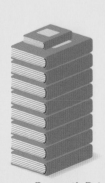

Lauran Bosworth Paine
1916–2001 **850 books**

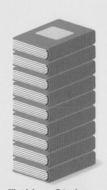

Kathleen Lindsay
1903–1973 **904 books**

Ryoki Inoue
1946– **1,086 books**

Edward Stratemeyer
1862–1930 **1,300 books**

Corin Tellado
1927–2009 **4,000 books**

= 100 books

Most prolific writers

FUN AND GAMES

Strap in, hold on and get ready to discover the adrenalin-fuelled world of the planet's top theme parks! They cater for millions of people and offer the most thrilling rides on Earth.

3 **Top Thrill Dragster**
Cedar Point, Sandusky, Ohio, USA
192 km/h

4 **Dodonpa**
Fuji-Q Highland, Yamanashi, Japan
171.2 km/h

=5 **Tower of Terror**
Dreamworld, Queensland, Australia
160 km/h

=5 **Superman: Escape from Krypton**
Six Flags Magic Mountain, Valencia, California, USA
160 km/h

Tallest rollercoaster

The tallest rollercoaster in the world is the Tower of Terror at Dreamworld amusement park in Queensland, Australia. It is 115.01 m tall – more than twice the height of **Nelson's Column**, London (52 m), and a little shorter than **St Peter's Basilica,** Rome (138 m).

10 **Leviathan**
Canada's Wonderland, Maple, Ontario, Canada
147.2 km/h

1 Formula Rossa
Ferrari World, Yas Island, Abu Dhabi
238.6 km/h

2 Kingda Ka
Six Flags Great Adventure, Jackson, New Jersey, USA
204.8 km/h

Ferrari World is the largest indoor amusement park in the world. It covers a total of 200,000 sq m and the indoor area is 86,000 sq m – as big as seven American football fields.

Ferrari World

Formula Rossa at Ferrari World in Abu Dhabi is the fastest rollercoaster in the world. It accelerates from **0–100 km/h in 2 seconds** – that's as fast as a Formula 1 car.

7 Ring racer
Nürburgring, Nürburg, Germany
159 km/h

8 Steel Dragon
Nagashima Spa Land, Nagashima, Japan
152 km/h

9 Millennium Force
Cedar Point, Sandusky, Ohio, USA
148.8 km/h

In total, the 10 most popular theme parks attract 126,669,000 people every year – that's more than the total population of Mexico.

71

THE SILVER SCREEN

Lights, camera, action! Since the first movies were made at the end of the 19th century, people have been producing films that continue to set records for money taken, number of people appearing, size and endurance!

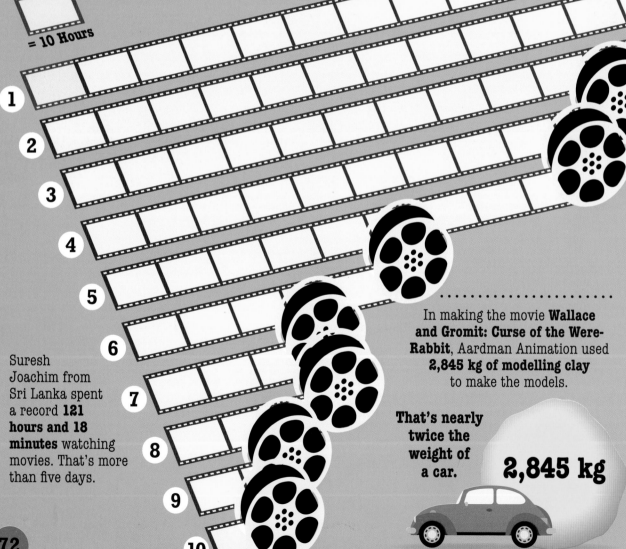

= 10 Hours

1
2
3
4
5
6
7
8
9
10

Suresh Joachim from Sri Lanka spent a record **121 hours and 18 minutes** watching movies. That's more than five days.

In making the movie **Wallace and Gromit: Curse of the Were-Rabbit**, Aardman Animation used **2,845 kg of modelling clay** to make the models.

That's nearly twice the weight of a car.

2,845 kg

GONE WITH THE WIND

CLARK GABLE
VIVIEN LEIGH
LESLIE HOWARD OLIVIA DE HAVILLAND

Highest-grossing film

When adjusted for inflation, the highest-grossing movie of all time is **Gone with the Wind.** Its adjusted figure comes in at **US$5,362,000,000.** In contrast, **Avatar** (2009), which holds the record for the highest-grossing movie (unadjusted) took **US$2.8 billion.**

Tiniest film

Measuring just **45 by 25 nanometres** a 60-second stop-motion film made by IBM is the smallest movie ever made. It was made using individual molecules, placing and moving them for each shot. The film tells the story of a boy playing with a ball.

Largest cast

More than **300,000 actors and extras** appeared in one scene for the movie **Gandhi** (1982), that is nearly the same size as the entire population of Iceland.

LONGEST FILMS EVER MADE

1. **Modern Times Forever (2011) – 14,400 minutes (240 hours OR 10 days)**

2. **Cinématon (1984) – 11,220 minutes (187 hours OR 7 days, 19 hours)**

3. **Beijing 2003 (2004) – 9,000 minutes (150 hours OR 6 days, 6 hours)**

4. **Matrjoschka (2006) – 5,700 minutes (95 hours OR 3 days 23 hours)**

5. **The Cure for Insomnia (1987) – 5,220 minutes (87 hours OR 3 days, 15 hours)**

6. **The Longest Most Meaningless Movie in the World (1970) – 2,880 minutes (48 hours)**

7. ****** (1967) – 1,500 minutes (25 hours)**

8. **The Clock (2010) – 1,440 minutes (24 hours)**

9. **A Journal of Crude Oil (2008) – 840 minutes (14 hours)**

10. **Tie Xi Qu: West of the Tracks (2003) – 551 minutes (9 hours, 11 minutes)**

TUNE TIME

These artists really are the top of the pops! They've sold more songs and records than anyone else, had their songs played more times, had more number ones and had longer recording careers than any other acts on the planet.

Top selling artists (digital singles)

The best-selling digital single ever is **Baby** by Justin Bieber. Released in 2010, the song has been downloaded more than 12 million times.

Artist	Sales
Rihanna	102m
Taylor Swift	96.5m
Katy Perry	83.5m
Lady Gaga	59m
Kanye West	48m

Most No. 1 Albums

Having sold more than 42 million copies since its release in 1982, **Thriller** by Michael Jackson is the best-selling album of all time.

10
**Bruce Springsteen
Elvis Presley
Barbara Streisand**

Most played tune

The Disney tune **It's a Small World** may be the most played tune in world. It's more than 50 years old and it is played continuously at all of the company's theme parks. It may have been played **more than 50 million times.**

During a 16-hour day, it's played 1,200 times.

74

Longest career

The record for the longest career as a recording artist belongs to Judy Robinson. She released her first record in **1926** and her last recording was made in **2003**.

77 years

Fastest selling

828,773

The American singer Beyoncé holds the record for the fastest selling digital album in the US. In **2015, it was downloaded 828,773 times** in just three days.

MOST SUCCESSFUL RECORDING ARTISTS OF ALL TIME
(WORLDWIDE SALES – MILLIONS)

1.	**The Beatles – 600**
2.	Elvis Presley – 500–600
3.	**Michael Jackson – 300–400**
4.	Madonna – 275–300
5.	**Elton John – 250–300**
6.	Led Zeppelin – 300–300
7.	**Pink Floyd – 200–250**
8.	Rihanna – 191–200
=9.	**Mariah Carey – 175-200**
=9.	Celine Dione – 175–200

Most records

In 1975, the British rock band Led Zeppelin became the first band to have six albums in the charts at the same time.

13
Jay Z

19
Beatles

Streaming music

Songs played on internet streaming services, such as Spotify, now account for **more than one-third** of the music industry's earnings.

Record piano players

In 2012, the record for the greatest number of musicians playing a piano was set when 103 people took it in turns to play part of Beethoven's *Ode to Joy* at a concert in Japan.

FIT FOR A KING

Royal palaces are some of the most opulent and imposing buildings on the planet. Inside, the rooms are decked out in the height of luxury.

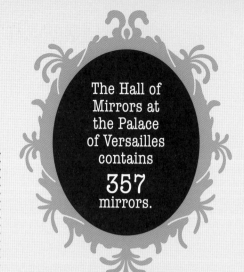

The Hall of Mirrors at the Palace of Versailles contains **357** mirrors.

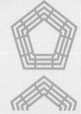

The enormous Louvre palace in Paris covers more than 1.5 times the area of the Pentagon building.

The Forbidden City

The Forbidden City in Beijing is part of a huge palace complex that covers **74 hectares** in total.

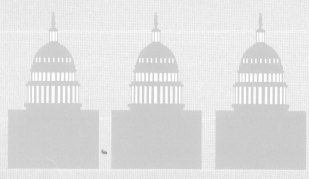

That's three times the area of the Capitol Building in Washington, DC, USA.

Palace of Parliament, Bucharest

It is the world's heaviest building, with **700,000 tonnes** of steel and bronze ...

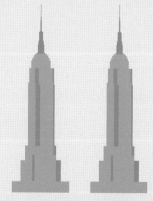

... that's twice the weight of the Empire State Building.

LARGEST ROYAL PALACES

1. **Louvre (Paris, France) – 210,000 sq m**
2. Istana Nurul Iman (Bandar Seri Begawan, Brunei) – 200,000 sq m
3. **Apostolic Palace (Vatican City) – 162,000 sq m**
4. Forbidden City (Beijing, China) – 150,000 sq m
5. **Royal Palace of Madrid (Madrid, Spain) – 135,000 sq m**
6. Quirinal Palace (Rome, Italy) – 110,500 sq m
7. **Buckingham Palace (London, UK) – 77,000 sq m**
8. Topkapi Palace (Istanbul, Turkey) – 70,000 sq m
9. **Palace of Versailles (Versailles, France) – 67,000 sq m**
10. Royal Palace of Stockholm (Stockholm, Sweden) – 61,120 sq m

It has 1 million cubic m of marble

– that's enough to fill

x 400
Olympic swimming pools

Inside, there are **3,500 tonnes** of glass, which is equivalent to the weight of ...

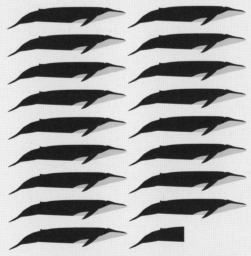

... 17.5 blue whales.

The glass is used in **1,409** lights and mirrors, and ...

... 480 chandeliers.

It has 200,000 sq m of carpet
– enough to cover ...

... 4 polo fields

ANCIENT BUILDINGS

The oldest surviving buildings in the world were built nearly 7,000 years ago. These ancient constructions are usually tombs, monuments or, like Stonehenge, puzzling structures whose real use remains a mystery.

Stonehenge

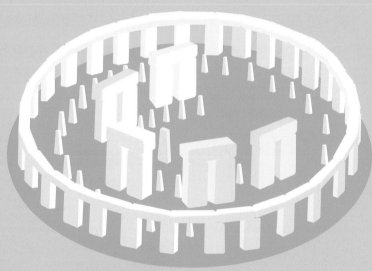

This ancient monument was started about **5,000 years** ago and built over a period of **1,000 years.**

Each stone weighs 22.5 tonnes ...

... as much as four elephants.

How it was built

Larger stones were levered into pits until they stood upright. Smaller stones were then raised using levers and platforms, before being pushed in place on top of the upright stones.

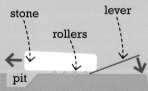

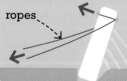

stone · rollers · lever · pit · ropes · logs

The larger stones were moved on rollers into place by a pit. One end of the stone was then raised using a lever.

Logs were placed under the raised end to keep it in place. The lever was used again to raise the stone even higher.

Ropes were then attached to lift the stone so that it was upright, with one end in the pit.

Finally, the pit was filled in, to hold the upright stone firmly in place.

OLDEST BUILDINGS IN THE WORLD

- =1. **Barnenez, France** – around 4800 BCE
- =1. **Tumulus of Bougon, France** – around 4800 BCE
- =1. **Tumulus Saint-Michel, France** – around 4800 BCE
- =4. **Wayland's Smithy, UK** – around 3700 BCE
- =4. **Knap of Howar, UK** – around 3700 BCE
- =4. **Ggantija, Malta** – around 3700 BCE
- 7. **West Kennet Long Barrow, UK** – around 3650 BCE
- 8. **Listoghil, Ireland** – around 3550 BCE
- =9. **Sechin Baho, Peru** – around 3500 BCE
- =9. **La Hougue Bie, Jersey** – around 3500 BCE

Great pyramids

Egypt has about **140 pyramids**, which were built as burial chambers for important people. They can be stepped, bent, or have a true, triangular shape.

These ancient buildings were constructed more than 4,500 years ago. The **Pyramid of Khufu** is the largest and it contains **2.3 million stones,** and weighs more than **5 million tonnes.**

It was originally 147 m tall and was the tallest building in the world for more than 3,500 years.

internal ramps

The heavy stones were dragged by teams of workers up ramps that wrapped around the pyramid.

ramp

True – Giza

Bent – Dahshur

Stepped – Saqqara

Pyramids of Queens

Pyramid of Menkaure

Pyramid of Khafre

Pyramid of Khufu

The pyramids of Giza

BRIDGING THE GAP

The world's greatest bridges are amazing feats of technology. They are capable of carrying thousands of tonnes of trucks, cars and buses over wide rivers, deep valleys and even whole stretches of ocean.

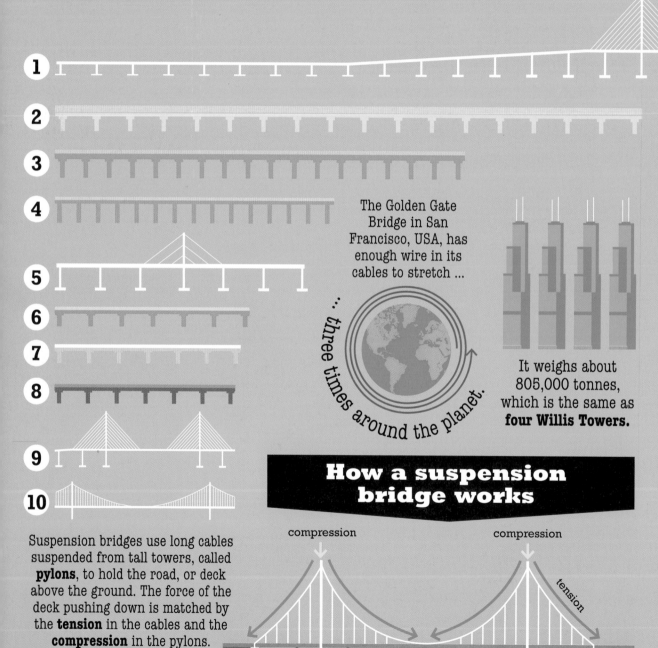

The Golden Gate Bridge in San Francisco, USA, has enough wire in its cables to stretch ...

... three times around the planet.

It weighs about 805,000 tonnes, which is the same as **four Willis Towers.**

How a suspension bridge works

compression

compression

tension

gravity

Suspension bridges use long cables suspended from tall towers, called **pylons**, to hold the road, or deck above the ground. The force of the deck pushing down is matched by the **tension** in the cables and the **compression** in the pylons.

The Millau Viaduct in France is the tallest bridge in the world, with a height of 343 m – taller than the **Eiffel Tower**.

343 m

The length of the world's longest bridge is greater than the distance between New York City and Philadelphia.

Driving across the world's longest bridge at 60 km/h, it would take a car **about 2 hrs 45 mins to complete the journey.**

LONGEST BRIDGES

1. **Danyang-Kunshan Grand Bridge (China)** – 164,800 m
2. **Tianjin Grand Bridge (China)** – 113,700 m
3. **Weinan Weihe Grand Bridge (China)** – 79,732 m
4. **Bang Na Expressway (Thailand)** – 54,000 m
5. **Beijing Grand Bridge (China)** – 48,153 m
6. **Lake Pontchartrain Causeway (USA)** – 38,442 m
7. **Manchac Swamp Bridge (USA)** – 36,710 m
8. **Yangcun Bridge (China)** – 35,812 m
9. **Hangzhou Bay Bridge (China)** – 35,673 m
10. **Runyang Bridge (China)** – 35,660 m

Widest Bridge

The world's widest bridge is the San Francisco-Oakland Bay Bridge in California, USA. It is **78.7 m** wide, which is more than 10 m wider than the wingspan of a **747-8 Jumbo Jet**.

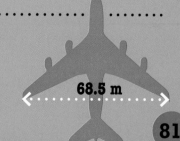

68.5 m

THAT DOESN'T LOOK RIGHT!

Some buildings are deliberately designed to look different, while others developed problems when they were built. The buildings shown here lean more than any others, some intentionally, while others have faults.

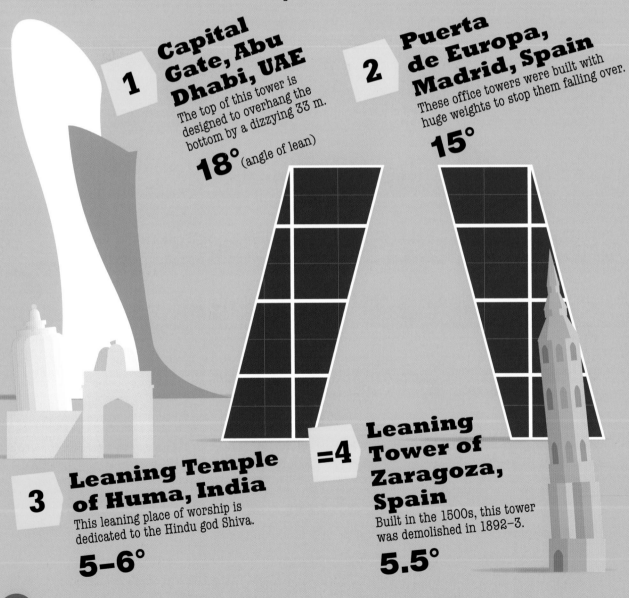

1 Capital Gate, Abu Dhabi, UAE
The top of this tower is designed to overhang the bottom by a dizzying 33 m.

18° (angle of lean)

2 Puerta de Europa, Madrid, Spain
These office towers were built with huge weights to stop them falling over.

15°

3 Leaning Temple of Huma, India
This leaning place of worship is dedicated to the Hindu god Shiva.

5–6°

=4 Leaning Tower of Zaragoza, Spain
Built in the 1500s, this tower was demolished in 1892–3.

5.5°

Melting building

sunlight

Nicknamed the 'Walkie-Talkie', the curved shape of this building in the City of London accidentally focusses sunlight on a spot in a nearby street. This creates temperatures of more than 90°C – that's hot enough to melt plastic surfaces on cars and even to fry an egg!

=4 Leaning Tower of Niles, Illinois, USA

Built in 1934, this is a half-sized replica of the Leaning Tower of Pisa.

5.5°

6 Leaning Tower of Suurhusen, Germany

The tower of this church started to lean when wooden beams rotted.

5.19°

7 Leaning Tower of Pisa

Built as a bell tower, this tower leans because it was built on soft ground and without adequate foundations.

3.99°

8 Tower of Garisenda, Bologna, Italy

This is the shorter of two leaning towers in Bologna, but it leans more than the other.

3.8°

=9 Leaning Tower of Nevyansk, Russia

The lean on this tower was caused by the ground beneath subsiding.

3°

=9 Yunyan Pagoda, China

Cracks in supporting pillars have caused this 47-m tower to lean to one side.

3°

Before the Burj Khalifa, the tallest artificial structure was a radio mast built near Warsaw in Poland. It was 646.38 m tall – lying down it would be as long as 45 double-decker buses. It collapsed on 8 August 1991.

SUPERDOMES

Because it has no sharp edges or flat surfaces, a dome is a very strong shape and can be used to cover a huge area. Domes are found on churches, markets and stadiums.

Strong domes

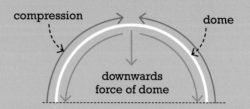

compression — dome

downwards force of dome

Domes work in the same way as arches. Weight from the top of the dome is distributed down its walls, creating a pressure (or compression) which pushes the dome together, making it even stronger.

St Paul's Cathedral

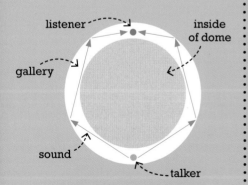

The dome of St Paul's, London, is one of the largest cathedral domes in the world. It weighs about **65,000 tonnes**, which is about the same as a large aircraft carrier.

listener — inside of dome

gallery

sound — talker

The first level of the dome is called the Whispering Gallery. The special acoustics mean that a whisper made on one side of the gallery can be heard on the other.

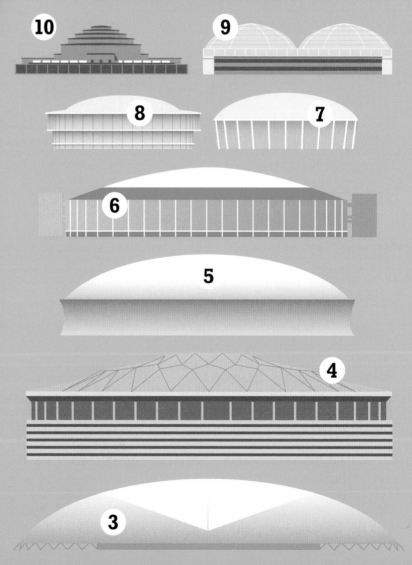

10

9

8

7

6

5

4

3

LARGEST DOMES THROUGH HISTORY

1. **New Singapore National Stadium, Singapore (2014–) – 312 m**
2. **Cowboys Stadium, USA (2009–2014) – 275 m**
3. **Oita Stadium, Japan (2001–2009) – 274 m**
4. **Georgia Dome, USA (1992–2001) – 256 m**
5. **Louisiana Superdome, USA (1975–1992) – 207 m**
6. **Astrodome, USA (1965–1975) – 195.5 m**
7. **Belgrade Fair – Hall 1, Serbia (1967–1965) – 109 m**
8. **Bojangles' Coliseum, USA (1955–1957) – 101.5 m**
9. **Leipzig Market Hall, Germany (1930–1955) – 65.5 m**
10. **Centennial Hall, Poland (1913–1930) – 65 m**

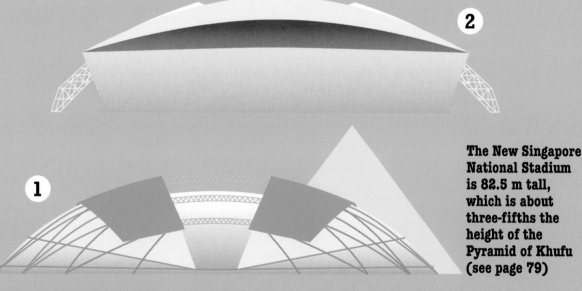

The New Singapore National Stadium is 82.5 m tall, which is about three-fifths the height of the Pyramid of Khufu (see page 79)

Geodesic domes

A geodesic dome combines arches and triangles to create a large, but lightweight covering.

The Fukuoka Yafuoku! Dome, Japan, is one of the largest geodesic domes in the world. This baseball stadium can seat **30,000 people** and it is 84 m tall, almost as tall as the **Statue of Liberty**.

93 m

ON THE MOVE

Millions of people travel around the globe every year, flying from huge airports or boarding trains from busy stations. At the same time, enormous cargo ships carry billions of tonnes of cargo to bustling ports and freight terminals.

= 5 million passengers

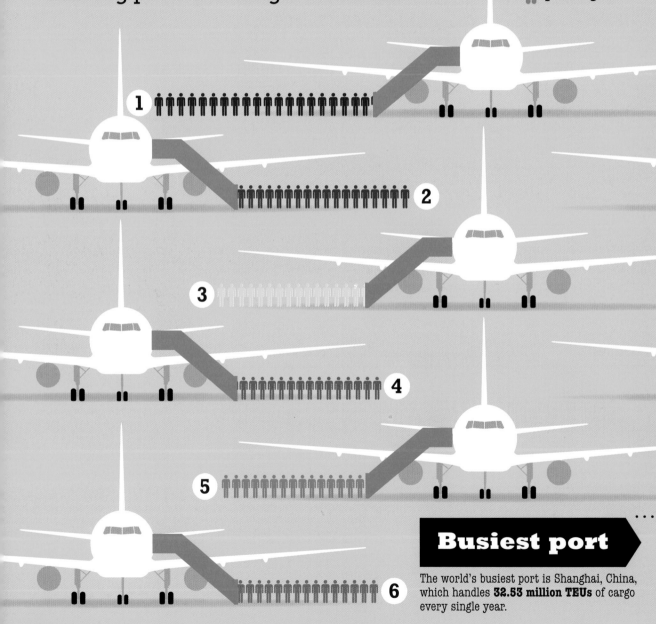

Busiest port

The world's busiest port is Shanghai, China, which handles **32.53 million TEUs** of cargo every single year.

BUSIEST AIRPORTS

1. **Atlanta, USA – 101,491,106 passengers per year**
2. Beijing, China – 90,203,000
3. **Dubai International Airport – 78,014,838**
4. Chicago O'Hare International Airport – 76,949336
5. **Tokyo, Japan – 75,300,000**
6. Heathrow, UK – 74,954,289
7. **Los Angeles, USA - 74,936,256**
8. Hong Kong, China – 68,488,000
9. **Paris (CDG), France – 65,766,986**
10. Dallas/Fort Worth, USA – 64,174,163

About 93 per cent of the passengers travelling through Heathrow airport are using international flights. That figure for Atlanta airport is around 10 per cent.

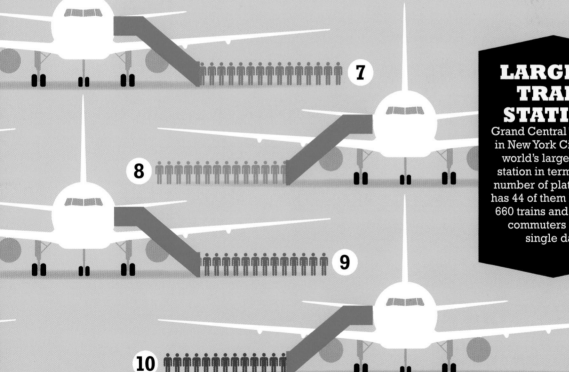

LARGEST TRAIN STATION

Grand Central Terminal in New York City is the world's largest train station in terms of the number of platforms. It has 44 of them handling 660 trains and 125,000 commuters every single day.

TEU stands for 'twenty-foot equivalent units', which is the size of a standard shipping container. One of these holds **38.5 cubic m**, which is about ...

250 full baths of water.

This means that Shanghai handles about **1.25 billion cubic m** of cargo every year, or **140,000 cubic m** every single hour (working 24 hours a day and 365 days a year!).

That's enough to fill 20 blimps.

BUILDING IN SPACE

<----------------------------------->

Space stations are designed to support a human crew for many months. They are just like homes in space, with facilities for sleeping, eating, washing and working.

1 International Space Station (ISS – various)

The ISS was built jointly by several countries.

907 m³ (volume of pressurised space)

2 Skylab (USA)

This orbited Earth from 1973 until it re-entered and burned up in Earth's atmosphere in 1979.

360 m³

3 Mir (USSR/ Russia)

This was the first space station that was built in stages and it orbited from 1986 to 2001.

350 m³

=4 Salyut 5 (USSR)

This space station was in orbit for just over a year, but was only occupied for 67 days.

100 m³

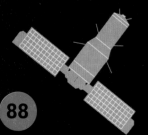

=4 Salyut 1 (USSR)

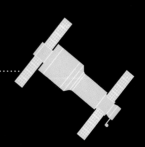

Launched in 1971, this was the first ever space station.

100 m³

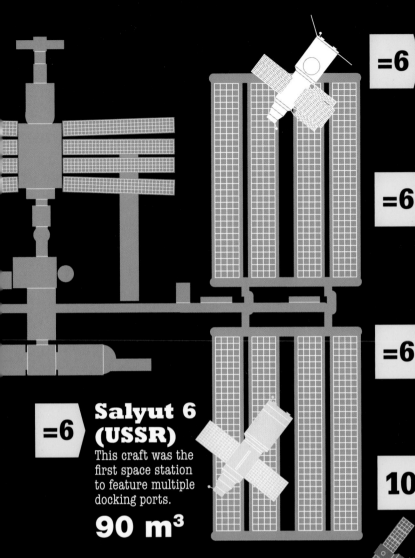

=6 Salyut 7 (USSR)

This was the last station that was part of the Salyut programme and was replaced by Mir.

90 m³

=6 Salyut 4 (USSR)

This space station made more than 12,000 orbits around Earth.

90 m³

=6 Salyut 3 (USSR)

This space station was occupied for just 15 days.

90 m³

=6 Salyut 6 (USSR)

This craft was the first space station to feature multiple docking ports.

90 m³

10 Tiangong 1 (China)

China's first space station. Its name means 'Heavenly Place'.

14.4 m³

ISS facts

The ISS weighs 419.455 tonnes – about the same as two blue whales.

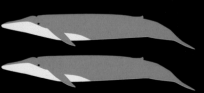

It was built in stages – different modules were launched into space and put together in orbit. The first module, called Zarya, weighed just 19.3 tonnes.

Zarya FGU

The huge solar arrays can produce 110 kw of total power, which is enough to power 55 homes.

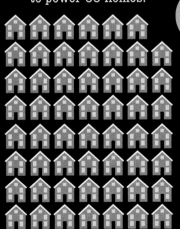

It orbits at a speed of 28,000 km/h, and it travels around about two-thirds of the planet every hour.

In a single day it travels the equivalent distance from Earth to the Moon and back.

The inside of the International Space Station has the same volume as a Boeing 747 Jumbo Jet – **enough to hold 19 million ping pong balls!** It contains laboratories, an observatory, toilets and washing facilities, and living quarters for the astronauts.

INTO SPACE

Humans have been exploring space for over 50 years, using robots or sending people. Launched in 1977, the spacecraft Voyager 1 has now travelled over 19 billion km – farther than any other human-made object.

Distance travelled by extraterrestrial rovers

Robot rovers have proved extremely useful in exploring other bodies in the Solar System. Many have lasted well beyond their scheduled mission, sending back vital information.

Sojourner (Mars) – 0.1 km
This small rover was active on the Martian surface from July to September 1997.

Spirit (Mars) – 7.7 km
This rover was active from 2004 until it became stuck in the Martian soil and lost contact in 2010.

Curiosity (Mars) – 8.6 km
Landing on Mars in 2012, Curiosity is about the size of a small car.

Lunokhod 1 (Moon) – 10.5 km
This Soviet craft was the first robot rover to explore another object in the Solar System. It operated from November 1970 to September 1971.

Eugene Cernan drove the Apollo 17 lunar rover to 17 km/h, setting a speed record for extraterrestrial rovers.

Moon rock

Between 1969 and 1972, the Apollo missions brought back **382 kg** of lunar rock samples – more than the weight of **five people**.

LONGEST HUMAN SPACE FLIGHTS

1. **Valeri Polyakov (Russia) 437.7 days (1994–5)**

2. Sergei Avdeyev (Russia) 379.6 days (1998–9)

3. **Vladimir Titov and Musa Manarov (USSR) 365.0 days (1987–8)**

4. Yuri Romanenko (USSR) 326.5 days (1987)

5. **Sergei Krikalev (USSR/Russia) 311.8 days (1991–2)**

6. Valeri Polyakov (USSR) 240.9 days (1988–9)

7. **Leonid Kizim, Vladimir Solovyov, Oleg Atkov (USSR) 237.0 days (1984)**

8. Mikhail Tyurin, Michale López-Alegría (Russia, USA) 215.4 days (2006–7)

9. **Anatoli Berezovoy, Valentin Lebedev (USSR) 211.4 days (1982)**

10. Talgat Musabayev, Nikolai Budarin (Russia) 207.5 days (1998)

Animals in Space

Animals sent into space include dogs, cats, chimpanzees, monkeys, spiders, frogs, fish, crickets and ants.

Tiny creatures called tardigrades (water bears) were even exposed to the freezing cold (**-272°C**) of space for 10 days and **survived**!

Apollo 16 rover (Moon) – 27.1 km
Astronauts John Young and Charles Duke drove this rover around the Moon in 1972.

Apollo 15 rover (Moon) – 27.8 km
David Scott and James Irwin used this rover during their three-day stay on the Moon in 1971.

Apollo 17 rover (Moon) – 35.74 km
The last Apollo rover was driven by Eugene Cernan and Harrison Schmitt in 1972.

Lunokhod 2 (Moon) – 39 km
This Soviet lunar rover was active from January to May 1973.

Opportunity (Mars) – 40.25 km
Identical to Spirit, this rover has remained active for more than 12 years.

Food in space

Astronauts' food is precooked or processed so that it does not require refrigeration. Astronauts have 1.7 kg of food to eat a day – the same weight as ...

... four cans of soup.

THE SOLAR SYSTEM

<·····················>

The family of planets, dwarf planets and small objects, such as asteroids, is called the Solar System. At its centre is a ball of burning gas; the Sun. So what are the largest objects in the Solar System?

6 Earth

Earth is the third planet from the Sun and it has one natural satellite, the Moon.

12,742 km

7 Venus

The second planet from the Sun has an atmosphere that's so thick that we cannot see the planet's surface.

12,104 km

8 Mars

Mars is called the red planet because its surface contains a lot of iron oxide, or rust.

6,780 km

9 Ganymede

Orbiting Jupiter, Ganymede is the largest moon in the Solar System and bigger than the planet Mercury.

5,268 km

10 Titan

Titan is Saturn's largest moon and its surface has seas, lakes and rivers of methane and ethane.

5,152 km

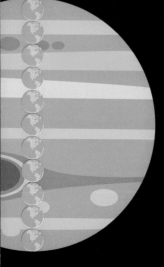

Giant planet

Jupiter has about 1,320 times the volume of Earth, its **diameter** is 11 times that of Earth and it has a surface area that is 120 times **bigger**.

However, it is only 317 times Earth's mass, because its density is one-quarter that of our planet.

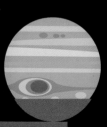

Goldilocks Zone

If a planet is too close to the Sun, then conditions are **too hot** for life to exist. Too far away, and conditions are **too cold**. In between is a region called the Goldilocks Zone, where conditions are **just right** for life.

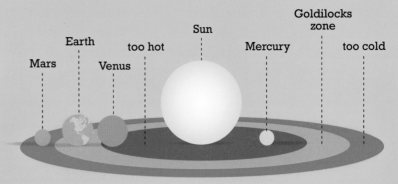

Mars Earth Venus too hot Sun Mercury Goldilocks zone too cold

4 Uranus

This planet is a bright blue colour because its atmosphere contains a lot of methane.

50,724 km

5 Neptune

This planet is almost the same size as Uranus, and it takes nearly 165 years to orbit the Sun.

49,244 km

3 Saturn

Saturn is surrounded by a bright ring system, which is made up of pieces of ice and rock.

116,464 km

2 Jupiter

The largest planet in the Solar System, Jupiter is the fifth planet from the Sun.

142,984 km

Sun facts

It makes up 99.8% of the entire Solar System's mass.
It will continue to shine for 5.5 billion years, before expanding beyond Earth's orbit and then shrinking to form a tiny white dwarf star.

1 Sun

The Sun produces light and heat by fusing together hydrogen atoms, which releases energy.

1,391,016 km

IN A SPIN

Every planet spins around on its axis, creating periods of day and night. Jupiter is the fastest spinning planet in the Solar System, and its day only lasts for 9.8 Earth hours.

PLANETS AND DWARF PLANETS WITH THE LONGEST DAYS (EARTH TIME)

1. **Venus – 245 days 0 hours 25 minutes 55 seconds**
2. Mercury – 58 days 15 hours 30 minutes 14 seconds
3. **Sun – 25 days 9 hours 7 minutes 26 seconds**
4. Pluto – 6 days 9 hours 17 minutes 17 seconds
5. **Eris – 1 day 1 hour 53 minutes 46 seconds**
6. Mars – 24 hours 37 minutes 26 seconds
7. **Earth – 23 hours 56 minutes 41 seconds**
8. Makemake – 22 hours 29 minutes 17 seconds
9. **Uranus – 17 hours 13 minutes 55 seconds**
10. Neptune – 16 hours 6 minutes 4 seconds

Lengths of the seasons

The planets move around the Sun in paths called **orbits**. Because the planets are **tilted**, different parts of each planet point towards the Sun at different parts of these orbits, creating the **seasons**. The length of the planets' seasons varies greatly depending on their **tilt** and the **length** of their orbit.

Mars
7 months

Earth
90–93 days

Venus
55–58 days

Jupiter
3 years

Saturn
7 years

Uranus
20 years

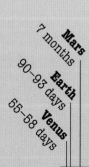

Changing shape

Jupiter's fast spin actually **squashes** the planet slightly, creating a shape called an oblate spheroid. It is more than **4,500 km wider** than it is **tall**.

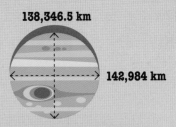

138,346.5 km

142,984 km

Axial tilt

The objects that make up the Solar System spin around at different angles, known as the **axial tilt**. The images here show the planets in the Solar System with the greatest axial tilt.

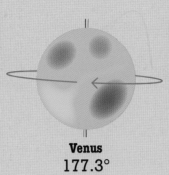

Venus
177.3°

Venus

The planet Venus actually spins in the **opposite direction** to the other planets – this is known as **retrograde spin**. If Earth rotated in the same direction as Venus, then the Sun would rise in the west and set in the east.

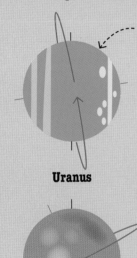

Uranus has its axis at an angle of 98° and spins on its side.

Uranus

Neptune
28.32°

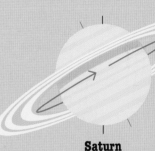

Saturn
26.7°

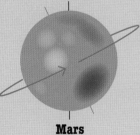

Mars
25°

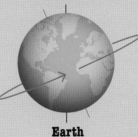

Earth
23.5°

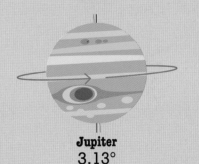

Jupiter
3.13°

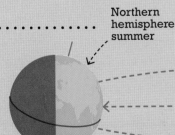

Northern hemisphere summer

Earth's orbit

Northern hemisphere winter

Southern hemisphere winter

Southern hemisphere summer

Neptune 40 years

ON THE SURFACE

The four planets closest to the Sun have rocky surfaces that are covered with towering peaks, huge chasms and the scars of impacts from asteroids and comets.

Olympus Mons

This Martian volcano covers the same area as Arizona, USA.

Arizona

Its peak is **three times** higher than Everest.

The six craters (calderas) at the summit are about 85 km wide – nearly twice the size of Greater London, UK, which is 48 km wide.

Greater London

Six craters

Valles Marineris

This huge canyon on Mars is up to 10 km deep. That's about 10 times the depth of the Grand Canyon.

It stretches around 20 per cent of the whole of **Mars**, and would stretch across **North America**.

The huge peak of Pavonis Mons on Mars measures 375 km across.

When measured from the sea floor, Mauna Kea is the tallest mountain on Earth and one of five volcanoes that make up the island of Hawaii, USA.

TALLEST MOUNTAINS IN THE SOLAR SYSTEM (HEIGHT)

1. **Olympus Mons (Mars) – 24.8 km**
2. Rheasilvia Mons (Vesta) – 21.1 km
3. **Equatorial Ridge (Iapetus) – 19.8 km**
4. Ascraeus Mons (Mars) – 18.1 km
5. **Boösaule Montes (Io) – 17.4 km**
6. Arsia Mons (Mars) – 15.8 km
7. **Pavonis Mons (Mars) – 13.9 km**
8. Elysium Mons (Mars) – 12.5 km
9. **Maxwell Montes (Venus) – 10.9 km**
10. Mauna Kea (Earth) – 9.1 km

A 100-km wide asteroid hit Mercury about 4 billion years ago, creating a huge crater called the Caloris Basin. This is 1,550 km wide and could contain the state of Texas, USA.

1 Olympus Mons is surrounded by a cliff that is about 10 km high.

3

5

8

Boösaule Montes is found on Jupiter's moon, Io, the most volcanically active body in the Solar System.

9

Maxwell Montes is a mountain range that is about 850 km long and 700 km wide.

DEEP IMPACT

The Solar System is not a safe place! Millions of pieces of rock and ice are flying around at enormous speeds. Sometimes, they slam into planets with devastating results.

Yucatán impact

About **66 million years ago,** an object about **10 km** across hit the Earth with the force of around **one billion atomic bombs.**

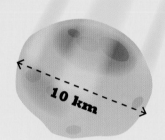

10 km

The object was travelling at a speed of nearly **30 km a second**. That's more than 150 times faster that a **jet airliner**.

Crater

Gulf of Mexico

Yucatán Peninsula

Mexico

At the moment of impact, the asteroid created a **crater** that was **100 km** across and about **30 km** deep.

100 km

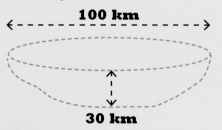

30 km

It's likely that the impact created an enormous **tsunami**, measuring **4–5 km** high – about 6.5 times the height of the **Burj Khalifa** (see page 56–7).

4–5 km

The collision threw up so much **dust and pollution** that scientists believe it blocked out the Sun for up to **six months**, leading to ...

... acid rain, ...

... collapse of photosynthesis ...

... and global temperature reduction.

This **change in conditions** was so great that it caused the **extinction** of the **dinosaurs**.

Shoemaker-Levy 9

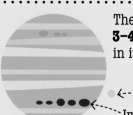

The largest piece was about **3–4 km** wide and left a hole in its atmosphere **twice the size of Earth.**

In 1994, fragments from comet Shoemaker-Levy 9 slammed into Jupiter with incredible force. The pieces were travelling at 216,000 km/h.

<--- Earth

Impact scars

BIGGEST CRATERS IN THE SOLAR SYSTEM (DIAMETER)

1. **Borealis Basin (Mars) – 8,500 km**
2. Valhalla (Callisto) – 4,000 km
3. **South Pole-Aitken Basin (Moon) – 2,500 km**
4. Hellas Basin (Mars) – 2,100 km
5. **Argyre Basin (Mars) – 1,800 km**
6. Caloris Basin (Mercury) – 1,550 km
7. **Isidis Planitia (Mars) – 1,500 km**
8. Asgard (Callisto) – 1,400 km
9. **Mare Imbrium (Moon) – 1,100 km**
10. Turgis (Iapetus) – 580 km

How the Moon was formed

About 4.6 billion years ago, an object the size of **Mars** slammed into **Earth**, creating a spray of debris that clumped together to form the **Moon**.

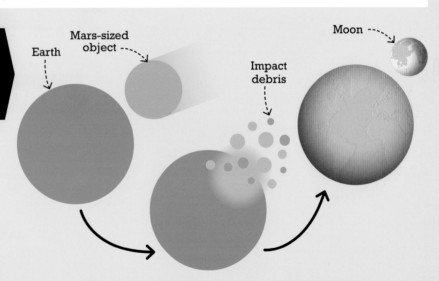

Earth

Mars-sized object

Impact debris

Moon

Chelyabinsk meteor

In 2013, a **20-m** wide piece of rock with a mass of **10,000 tonnes** entered Earth's atmosphere and exploded in the air over Russia.
The explosion injured 1,200 people.
It had a force equivalent to about
500 kilotonnes of TNT – nearly **30 times** the force of the atomic bomb dropped on Hiroshima.

SMALL BODIES

<·······························>

Comets and asteroids may be small compared with the planets, but they can cause spectacular events, including glowing comet tails and shooting stars. The Solar System is populated with millions of these small bodies.

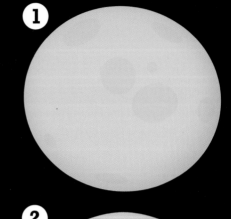

1

2

3

4

5

6

7

8

9

10

Dwarf planet

The largest object in the Asteroid Belt is called **Ceres**. It has a diameter of **950 km** and was first spotted in 1801. It was initially classified as an **asteroid**, but in 2006, it was re-classified as a **dwarf planet**. A dwarf planet is an object that **orbits** the Sun, is **roughly** round in shape, but hasn't cleared its orbit of **other objects**.

On its own, Ceres accounts for 25 per cent of the Asteroid Belt's total mass.

LARGEST ASTEROIDS (DIAMETER)

1. 2 Pallas – 545 km
2. 4 Vesta – 530 km
3. 10 Hygiea – 407 km
4. 511 Davida – 326 km
5. 704 Interamnia – 316 km
6. 52 Europa – 302 km
7. 87 Sylvia – 260 km
=8. 31 Euphrosyne – 255 km
=8. 15 Eunomia – 255 km
10. 16 Psyche – 253 km

Most asteroids are found in a zone between Mars and Jupiter known as the Asteroid Belt. Scientists believe that the belt has more than 750,000 asteroids that are larger than 1 km across.

Comet probe

In November 2014, the probe **Philae** landed on the 4-km-wide comet 67P/Churyumov-Gerasimenko after a journey of **6.4 billion km**.

Comet facts

Comet particles that are bigger than **2 mm** burn up at 1,600°C as they enter the atmosphere, creating **shooting stars**.

Actual size

Every day, about 300 tonnes of dust, much of it from comets, reaches Earth – about the weight of **1.5 blue whales**.

2 mins

Comet particles stream out at speeds of **350 km** a second. That is quick enough to travel around Earth in **less than two minutes**.

Comet tails

In 2007, the tail of Comet McNaught was measured at more than **224 million km long**.

That's about 1.5 times the distance from Earth to the Sun.

 ←----- 149,600,000 km ----→

DISTANT WORLDS

<----------------------------------->

Until recently, no-one had discovered planets outside our Solar System. However, in the last 25 years, hundreds of these exoplanets have been found circling other stars, and some of these are the largest planets ever discovered.

The exoplanet known as Kepler 42c completes an orbit around its star in just 4.3 hours.

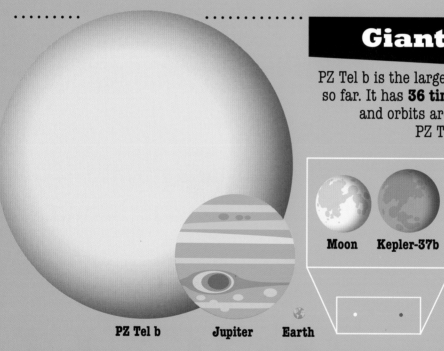

Giant planet

PZ Tel b is the largest **exoplanet** discovered so far. It has **36 times** the mass of Jupiter and orbits around a star called PZ Telescopii.

Moon **Kepler-37b**

PZ Tel b **Jupiter** **Earth**

Kepler-37b

One of the smallest known exoplanets is Kepler-37b. It is about the size of the Moon, has a year that lasts just 13 days and has a surface temperature of 425°C.

PZ Tel b orbits its star at 18 times the distance from the Sun to Earth. Astronomers call this Sun–Earth distance an **astronomical unit** (AU).

PZ Telescopii and its giant planet lie about **175 light years** from Earth, and can be seen in the constellation Telescopium.

<----------------------- 18 AU

<- 1 AU

Discovered in 2013, **Kepler-78b** is the same size as Earth, but it orbits its star in 8.5 hours and has a surface temperature of **2,826°C** – hot enough to melt iron!

Red-hot world

LARGEST EXOPLANETS
(TIMES EARTH)

1. **PZ Tel b – 27.1**
2. **CT Cha b – 24.64**
3. **HAT-P-32 b – 22.81**
4. **WASP-17 b – 22.3**
=5. **KOI-368.01 b – 20.5**
=5. **WASP-76 – 20.5**
7. **HAT-P33 b – 20.46**
8. **GQ Lup b – 20.16**
9. **WASP-78 b – 19.6**
10. **WASP-12 b – 19.44**

How many?

As many as one in five sun-like stars have an Earth-sized planet in the habitable Goldilocks Zone (see page 93). These planets may have the right conditions for life to exist.

20%

How exoplanets are discovered

Exoplanets are usually too dim to be seen directly, so **astronomers** look out for the effects they might have on other objects, such as the light from the stars they orbit or from other objects that are **farther away**.

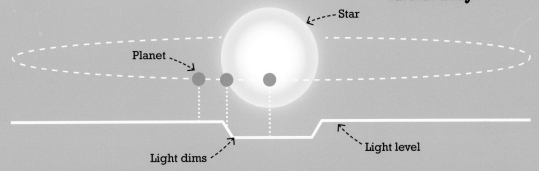

As the exoplanet travels **in front** of its star, it causes the star's light to **dim** slightly. Astronomers can use this method to calculate the **size** of the exoplanet.

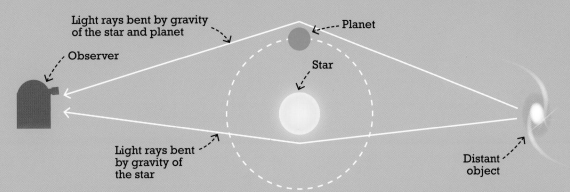

A star's **gravity** actually bends the light coming from a more distant object that's far **behind** it. If that star has a planet orbiting it, then the gravity of the planet will cause the light to bend **even more,** distorting the image of the distant object.

STAR LIGHT, STAR BRIGHT

The Sun is one of billions of stars that form our galaxy, which is called the Milky Way. This chart shows the 10 stars and star systems that are closest to us and their distance in light years (ly).

9 **Epsilon Eridani**
This orange dwarf star has a large, Jupiter-sized planet orbiting it.
10.52 ly

15 light years

10 light years

5 light years

4 **Lalande 21185**
Visible with the help of binoculars, this small red star is up to 10 billion years old.
8.29 ly

3 **Wolf 359**
This very dim red star was first seen in 1916.
7.78 ly

Dense stars

Neutron stars are so dense that a teaspoon full of their matter would have a mass of **1 billion tonnes** –

equivalent to more than **1,500** fully laden supertankers.

5 **Sirius**
This system contains two stars, Sirius A and Sirius B. Sirius A is the brightest star in our night sky.
8.58 ly

1 **Alpha Centauri**
This system is made up of three stars, the closest of which is called Proxima Centauri.
4.24-4.37 ly

This is the distance light travels in one year. Light travels at 300,000 km a second (about 7.5 times around Earth).

7.5

That's equivalent to 9,460,528,400,000 km in a whole year!

8 **Ross 248**
This is a single, small, dim red star.
10.32 ly

Types of star

Astronomers classify stars in spectral types, depending on their colour, make-up and the temperature at which they burn. Each type is given a letter.

O-class stars are blue and have a temperature of up to 50,000°C.

B-class stars are blue-white and have a temperature of up to 28,000°C.

A-class stars are white and have a temperature of up to 10,000°C.

F-class stars are pale yellow and have a temperature of up to 7,500°C.

G-class stars, such as our Sun, are yellow and have a temperature of up to 6,000°C.

K-class stars are orange and have a temperature of up to 4,900°C

M-class stars are red and have a temperature of up to 3,500°C.

2 **Barnard's Star**
This small star is very dim and is not visible to the naked eye from Earth.
5.96 ly

6 **Luyten 726**
This system is made up of two small red stars that are slowly orbiting each other.
8–8.73 ly

7 **Ross 154**
This is a single red star.
9.68 ly

10 **Lacille 9352**
Even though this is a red star, it is quite bright and can be seen using binoculars.
10.74 ly

SIZE OF THE UNIVERSE

Space is enormous, which is why distances between stars and galaxies are measured in light years. These images show some of the biggest astronomical bodies in our Solar System, our galaxy, and beyond.

1 ## Supercluster

These are some of the largest structures in the Universe. The Virgo Supercluster is made up of more than 100 groups of galaxies, called clusters.

110 million ly

2 ## Galaxy cluster

Galaxies join together to form clusters. The Virgo Cluster contains up to 2,000 galaxies.

5 million ly

3 ## Galaxy

Stars join together to create galaxies. They can vary greatly in size and shape, but galaxy NGC 6872 is one of the biggest and contains up to 2 trillion stars

522,000 ly

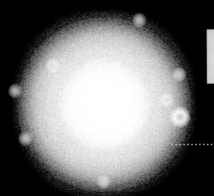

Star cluster

4

Within galaxies, stars move about in groups called clusters. One of the biggest in our galaxy is a globular cluster called Omega Centauri.

230 ly

Star

5

One of the largest stars in our galaxy is VY Canis Majoris. It is more than 2,000 times the size of our Sun.

1.4 billion km

Planet

6

Jupiter is the largest planet in our Solar System. It is a huge ball of gas with a solid core.

142,984 km

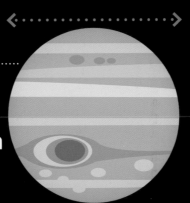

Dwarf planet

7

Ceres is one of the largest dwarf planets in our Solar System. It orbits the Sun in an area called the Asteroid Belt.

950 km

Moon

8

Moons are natural satellites that orbit around planets. The largest in our Solar System is Ganymede.

5,268 km

Asteroid

9

The Asteroid Belt lies between Mars and Jupiter and contains millions of rocks. The largest of these asteroids is Pallas.

545 km

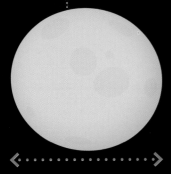

Comet

10

A comet's nucleus is a 'dirty snowball' of ice and dust. Comet Hale-Bopp has the largest known nucleus.

100 km

GLOSSARY

acid rain
Rain with a high concentration of harmful, poisonous chemicals that can cause the rain to act like an acid, eroding things it lands on.

acoustics
The science of how sound waves behave as they travel through objects, including air.

acrylic
A type of plastic that is both lightweight and strong.

barrow
An ancient burial mound.

blimp
A type of airship.

breeding season
A period during the year when animals look and compete for mates and to have young.

carbon dioxide
A colourless, odourless gas present in the atmosphere.

cartilage
A flexible tissue that supports some body parts, such as the human nose and ear, or, in some cases, is used to support the entire body, such as sharks and other cartilaginous fish.

cells
The smallest parts of a body. There are many different types of cell, and they combine in different ways to form all the body's structures.

circulatory system
A collection of organs, tissues and cells – including the heart and blood vessels – which helps to transport blood, and the oxygen and nutrients it contains, around the body.

circumference
The distance around the edge of a circle or curved shape.

decibel
The unit used to measure the intensity or volume (loudness) of sound.

diameter
The width of a circle or sphere measured through its centre point.

digestive system
A network of organs, tissues and cells that work together to take in food, extract its nutrients and expel any waste products.

drag
The force that slows down objects as they move through air or water.

dynamic apnea
A type of diving where people see how far they can go underwater just by holding their breath and not by using any special breathing apparatus.

enzyme
A type of protein produced by the body which aids certain chemical reactions.

extinction
When a type of living thing dies out completely and is no longer present.

globular cluster
A large, dense ball of stars that orbits around the centre of a galaxy.

gross domestic product
The total value of the amount of goods and services produced by a country over the course of a year.

hectare
A unit used to measure land area. One hectare equals 10,000 sq m.

immune system
A collection of organs, tissues and cells that help to protect the body from infection and disease.

inflation
When something increases in price.

leasable area
The amount of space in a building that can be leased, or rented, for shops or offices.

life expectancy
The average age a person can expect to live to.

light year
A unit of measurement equal to the distance light travels in a year: around 9.6 trillion kilometres.

mass
The amount of matter in a body or bodies, measured in kilograms.

migrate
To move from one place to another. Animals migrate to avoid harsh conditions, to search for food and water, or to go somewhere suitable to raise young.

module
A part or set of parts that can be joined with others to create a larger structure.

motor neurone
A type of long cell that runs through the spine and carries messages to the body's muscles in the form of tiny electrical signals.

nanometre
A tiny unit of measurement equal to just one billionth of a metre.

organ
A part of the body that carries out certain tasks or functions. The brain, heart and liver are all organs.

oxygen
Making up around 20 per cent of Earth's atmosphere, oxygen is a colourless, odourless gas.

photosynthesis
The process via which plants use the energy from sunlight to convert carbon dioxide and water from the ground into food, and produce oxygen as a waste product.

predator
An animal that hunts other animals to eat.

pressurised space
In a space station, this is the part of the craft where the atmosphere is under pressure and breathable and where astronauts can survive without wearing a spacesuit.

pylon
A tall vertical structure. In a suspension bridge, the pylons are the tall towers that support the long cables carrying the deck.

relic
The ancient remains of a saint or someone who was considered important.

radula
A tooth-like structure found in molluscs, such as snails, that is used for tearing and scraping food.

shooting star
A streak of light across the night sky, usually formed when a small piece of rock from an asteroid or a comet burns up in Earth's atmosphere.

skeletal muscle
Muscles that are attached to the skeleton and give the body its shape. They can be consciously controlled and moved via messages from the brain.

solar array
The parts of a spacecraft that produce electricity from sunlight.

Solar System
The Sun plus all the objects that orbit it, including planets, dwarf planets, asteroids and comets.

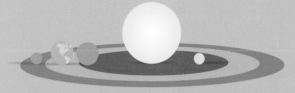

species
A group of organisms that share the same characteristics and are capable of breeding to produce fertile offspring.

streamlined
When something has a shape that helps it to move through air or water as easily as possible.

suspension bridge
A type of bridge that uses long cables hanging from towers to carry a deck that is suspended above the ground.

tumulus
A large mound of earth, rock and stones that has been built over a grave. The word is the Latin for 'small hill'.

ultrasound
Sounds that are so high-pitched that they cannot be heard by humans.

USSR
Short for the Union of Soviet Socialist Republics, this was the name given to the communist state made up of Russia and its neighbouring countries.

volume
The amount of physical space taken up by a solid body, liquid or gas. Volume is measured in cubic centimetres.

white dwarf
A small, hot star formed when a larger star collapses in on itself towards the end of its life.

INDEX

WEBSITES

‹••••••••••••••••••••••••••›

www.guinnessworldrecords.com
The website for all things about record-breaking. It is packed
with thousands of world records and facts.

www.visualinformation.info
A website that contains a whole host of infographic material on
subjects from natural history and science to sport and
computer games.

www.coolinfographics.com
A collection of infographics and data visualisations from other
online resources, magazines and newspapers.

www.dailyinfographic.com
A comprehensive collection of infographics on an enormous
range of topics that is updated every day!